98 NOT OUT

By the same author

Labour and Liberalism (1910)
Socialism for Pacifism (1917)
India and its Government (1921)
English Prisons Today (with Stephen Hobhouse, 1922)
A New Way with Crime (1928)
The Indian Crisis (1930)
Hungry England (1932)
The Bloody Traffic (1933)
Will Roosevelt Succeed? (1934)
Purple Plague: A Tale of Love and Revolution (1935)
Workers' Front (1938)
Inside the Left: Thirty Years of Platform, Press, Prison and Parliament, A Political Autobiography (1942)
Death Pays a Dividend (with Frederic Mullally, 1944)
German Diary (1946)
Socialism Over Sixty Years: The Life of Jowett of Bradford (1946)
Bermondsey Story: The Life of Alfred Salter (1949)
African Journeys (1955)
Red Liner: A Novel in TV Form (1961)
Outside the Right (1963)
African Socialism: A Background Book (1964)
Immigration: What is the Answer? Two Opposing Views (with Norman Pannell, 1965)
Woman Against the Desert (with Wendy Campbell-Purdie, 1967)
The Shrinking Explosive World (1967)
The Colonial Revolution (1973)
Towards Tomorrow (1977)
Britain's First Socialists (1980)

Fenner Brockway

98 NOT OUT

Quartet Books
London New York

Dedicated to Margaret Glover, my partner for peace

First published by Quartet Books Limited 1986
A member of the Namara Group
27/29 Goodge Street, London WIP 1FD

British Library Cataloguing in Publication Data

Brockway, Fenner
98 not out.
1. World Disarmament Campaign (UK) - History
I. Title
327.1'74'0924 JX1974

ISBN 0-7043-2589-6

Typeset by AKM Associates (UK) Ltd
Ajmal House, Hayes Road, Southall, London
Printed and bound in
Great Britain by Nene Litho
and Woolnough Bookbinding
both of Wellingborough, Northants

Contents

Acknowledgements

The author wishes to thank Margaret Glover for an exchange of ideas about this book during the five years that, on and off, he has been writing it; and for help in research and liaising with the publishers. He also wishes to thank Miss Mercy Edgedale who did the bulk of the typing for the book.

List of Illustrations

Neil Kinnock having descended from the platform to greet Fenner Brockway at the 1984 Labour Party Conference (photograph courtesy *The Times* Newspapers Ltd)

Indira Gandhi by Margaret Glover, the last portrait of the Indian Prime Minister before her assassination

Tony Banks, last Chairman of the GLC, greeting Fenner Brockway and Joan Hymans at a GLC reception

Fenner Brockway and Dora Russell in Cornwall, June 1985 (photograph courtesy Margaret Glover)

Fenner Brockway with youngest ILEA pupil, demonstrating support for ILEA, June 1985 (photograph courtesy ILEA *Contact*)

Fenner Brockway at the unveiling by Michael Foot of his statue in Red Lion Square, August 1985 (photograph courtesy John Chapman)

Fenner Brockway with his grandson David Brockway (photograph courtesy Christopher Brockway)

Fenner Brockway dons a Gandhi cap at the Indian National Congress Centenary Plenary Session, December 1985 (photograph courtesy Bombay *Free Press Journal*)

Foreword

Bernard Shaw once said to me: 'If I ever meet the Almighty I will tell Him that He is in my debt. By my work I have left the world a more enlightened place than He bestowed on me at birth.'

I don't feel a bit like that. Life has given me much more than I have given to life. I have been very fortunate.

I have known many of the most creative persons of my time, from H.G. Wells and Bernard Shaw to Bertrand Russell and Mahatma Gandhi.

I have had the friendship of a host of people, unknown but splendid. I have had the love and partnership of devoted women. I have had the affection and fun of children.

I have travelled over a great part of the world, seen its beauties, and learned to identify myself with all races.

I have always done what I wanted to do. Jobs have somehow followed my convictions. The one doubt has been the House of Lords.

I have had opportunity to devote myself to the causes in which I have believed.

I have seen the achievement of many aims: the welfare state, women's enfranchisement, the colonial political revolution and the growth of the peace movement.

I have had spiritual experiences which have revealed to me the meaning of life and given inspiration in activity.

In these last years I have had help, comfort and great happiness.

What more could anyone need or desire?

In what follows I have tried to reflect these experiences and to suggest what has still to be done.

1

Creators of Our Time

I have been remarkably privileged in knowing many of the creative personalities of this century. This was particularly so in the formative years when I was young and they influenced me greatly.

The first was Keir Hardie, the father of the modern Labour movement. I have told, elsewhere, how I went to see him for a journalistic interview when I was a young Liberal, and how he talked to me for an hour, and how I left him a young Socialist. Sylvia Pankhurst was present at his flat when I visited him. They did not hide their affection for each other. Sylvia sat on his knees, her arm round his neck. Later, Sylvia opened a nursery school in the East End to which my daughter Audrey went for a time. Keir Hardie had a remarkable physical presence. I can see him now as he opened the door of his Neville's Court flat - his towering head over his square body, like a granite statue. He adopted me as a political pupil, and guided me specially towards women's equality and opposition to imperialism and war. He died a victim of the war as much as any soldier in the trenches. He was broken in spirit, when the workers of different countries took up arms to kill each other at the command of capitalist governments.

The second was Bernard Shaw. A reply he gave me after a lecture at our Independent Labour Party (ILP) branch had the effect on me of a religious conversion. I asked him what we youngsters were to do with our lives. Head erect (his hair still a little ginger), his slim body straight, his arms folded, he answered decisively: 'Find out what the Life Force - the Creative Force - is making for in your time, and make for it too. Then you become greater than yourselves. You become a part of Creative Evolution.' That became my dynamic philosophy throughout my subsequent life. If Hardie adopted me as a political pupil, G.B.S. adopted me as an intellectual pupil. I have described elsewhere how I had the good fortune to be continually associated with him. Shaw destroyed for me all the shams of the Establishment. He made my Socialism apply to everything in life.

The third was H.G. Wells, who attended our ILP summer schools at Lady Warwick's Easton Lodge, not far from his home at Dunmow. He lectured, joined discussions, danced at our socials and took part in our games. He took to me when I defended him against Oswald Mosely, who was then a member of the ILP, and invited me to his home, and we met often before and after the 1914 war. Wells influenced my thinking profoundly by the knowledge he gave me of world politics. He helped to make me an international Socialist.

There were the Webbs. For a time Beatrice joined the ILP during the First World War. I remember her sitting in the first row at our annual conference, listening anxiously. I think she found us too emotional. In 1919 she invited me to become joint Secretary of the Prison System Enquiry Committee. I went to see her in the flat she and Sidney shared on the Embankment near the Tate Gallery. She sat on a legless chair with her feet stretched out on the floor while silent Sidney worked at a desk in the corner. 'We want facts, *facts*, FACTS,' she cried characteristically. On the committee she was friendly and immensely helpful. I liked and admired her.

Then there was Bertrand Russell. He was an example to me of courageous integrity. He completely threw in his lot with those of us who refused to be conscripted into the military forces in the First World War and lost his post at Cambridge University for so doing. When the editor of our paper was charged with publishing a seditious article, he wrote to *The Times* that he was the author and was imprisoned for six months. Bertrand did not look like a distinguished person. He was small and dressed shabbily. Nevertheless, he was attractive to women and fell in love frequently. Russell had an effect on my thinking when, after the Soviet Revolution, he warned that its totalitarianism could lead to the repression of personal liberty. In later life we were of course closely associated in challenging nuclear weapons.

George Orwell added to Russell's emphasis on the need to build a Socialism which recognized personal liberty. He was attracted to the ILP by its ethical approach to social change, but, when he came to see me before going to Spain to fight against Franco, he said he had been disillusioned by the bitter controversy between the pro-Communists and Trotskyists. However, he joined the ILP contingent. He had to flee finally not from Franco but from the Stalinists. Orwell was a gentle idealist. His warning of authoritarianism made me call myself a libertarian Socialist.

Clem Attlee made me realize how those with upper-class upbringings could identify themselves with the working class. It must have been about 1908 that I went to speak for the Limehouse ILP. In their branch rooms, behind a very proletarian group, a young man stood modestly, professionally clothed, wearing a white collar. After the meeting we had coffee together in a scrubby café. With difficulty I got him to talk about himself. He had been impressed at the Haileybury school mission by the ability of his working-class students, had been converted to Socialism by the Fabian Essays, had been repulsed by Fabian disbelief that the workers could form a political party, and had joined the ILP. That was Clem's beginning in the Labour Movement.

At the beginning of this century there was a remarkable group of women who, despite the absence of votes, influenced public events. They included Margaret Macmillan, who pioneered nursery schools (with whom my first wife co-operated), Margaret Bondfield, who became Britain's first woman Cabinet Minister, Mary Macarthur, who first organized women in trade unions, and Margaret MacDonald who, as Chairperson of the Women's Labour League, did much to win women to Socialism. Ramsay MacDonald's later years would, I believe, have been different if she had lived. I knew these women and they influenced me much in my lifelong activity for women's equality. With Mary Macarthur I co-operated in the establishment of Wages Councils for sweated workers by providing evidence of the condition of women home workers from knowledge gained at a settlement in an Islington slum. In the campaign for votes for women I first met Catherine Marshall who, as Parliamentary Secretary of the National Union of Women's Suffrage Societies, probably did more than anyone to win the vote. She secured the support of a large majority of MPs and candidates. I learned much from her of the techniques of parliamentary pressure.

My association with Rosa Luxemburg began before World War One. Although we never met, she became my political and personal heroine. She wrote and asked if I could help get a young woman, hiding from the threat of political arrest, out of Germany; we succeeded in smuggling her to Sweden. That began an exchange of letters between Rosa and myself which made us pen-friends. Her letters showed that she was a lovely character, humane and kind. I remember her telling me how in prison she had saved crumbs from her starvation diet for a visiting robin. She succeeded in reaching me even during the First World War, enclosing messages from Karl Liebknecht and Clara Zetkin. When I visited Berlin in 1946 I stood in reverence before the steps of the Eden Hotel where she and Liebknecht were assassinated. All history would have been different if Lenin had listened to Rosa's appeal to democratize the Bolshevik regime.

I must add a strange experience. A few years after the First World War I lectured at a seminar near Warsaw organized by the American Friends Service Committee. The caretaker, a grand figure of a man, brought me two books about Rosa Luxemburg, saying, 'You were her friend.' He was associated with Rosa closely and was the organizer of the Kiev naval mutiny which did much to bring the war to an end. He was unknown but deserved to be recognized as heroic no less than his and my heroine.

After the war we had in the ILP two successive chairmen who were certainly creative personalities. Clifford Allen had become prominent as chairman during the war of the No-Conscription Fellowship. He was unique in my experience. One does not often describe a man as beautiful but his features were that. He had an extraordinary spiritual influence, captivating audiences not by rhetoric but by creating a sense that every word came from his inner being. He was a genius in organization and transformed Socialism from a distant aim to a reliable objective. He influenced my thinking deeply and made Socialism a positive, attainable purpose.

James Maxton ousted Allen because of Allen's tolerance towards Ramsay MacDonald. Maxton was a creative personality, probably converting more people to Socialism than anyone. He was an extraordinary orator, always speaking of the fundamental principles of the new society. He could make his audiences roar with laughter at one moment and the next bring tears to their eyes by reciting a tragic event. He had a dramatic appearance, with long black hair descending down one cheek. He was loved by the ILP membership for his comradely equality and in the House of Commons drew crowded houses by his speeches and personality.

I was in contact with many leading European figures through my membership of the Executive of the Socialist International. I never met Jean Jaurès, but I shall never forget his speech at the great ILP demonstration in the Albert Hall a few months before his assassination at the beginning of the First World War. He spoke in French but we all understood what he was saying when he rose from stooping on the floor to standing with his arms above his head to depict the rise of the working class to Socialism.

At the International Executive I met Léon Blum, France's Popular Front Prime Minister, a forceful personality whose speeches always contained half a dozen perorations. The leader who impressed me most was Otto Bauer of Austria, Left in views, but who always succeeded in rewording my ILP motions so that they would be acceptable. When the ILP became associated with parties midway between the Social Democratic and Communist Internationals, among many picturesque figures I remember Joaquin Maurin, the leader of the Spanish POUM. He was reported shot when imprisoned by the Communists and when his wife addressed an ILP summer school I paid a tribute to him. Afterwards she told me confidentially that another prisoner had been shot mistakenly for him and that he was still alive. This was being kept secret.

I have known most prominent Members of Parliament in more recent years. I was a devotee of Nye Bevan. During the Second World War he used to attend gatherings of ILP leaders at a flat in Doughty Street where I had a room, perhaps more attracted by Jennie Lee, our young Scottish representative, than by our views. He subsequently married her. Although he supported the war he had considerable sympathy with ILP criticism.

When elected to Parliament in 1950 I used to be one of a group of about a dozen who sat and discussed things with him in a corner of the smoking-room. We were deeply disappointed when Nye supported the retention of the atom bomb in 1957 and the group in the smoking-room fell to two or three. Jennie was bitterly disappointed by how our comradeship broke. It should not have done so. Nye would have made a wonderful Foreign Secretary. I spent a weekend at his farm in Buckinghamshire. He was proud of his little stock.

In the House of Lords I was fortunate to have a few months with Lord Boyd Orr, whose service for world harmony I revered, and I became a close friend of Ritchie Calder, his able disciple. Disciple? He was a great creator himself. His book, *Man Against the Desert*, first awakened me to the way in which the earth's food problem could be solved.

Of all my colleagues, Philip Noel-Baker became closest to me. I had known him since 1919. He commanded the Friends Ambulance Corps in the war and what he saw meant that he dedicated the rest of his life to peace. I describe elsewhere how Philip and I came to start the World Disarmament

Campaign. We were inseparable comrades in this. His speeches in the Lords were amazing. Nearly blind, at first with a few bold notes, later with none, he held the House in silent absorption while, with his astonishing memory, he poured out facts and figures clothed in continuous rhetoric. I saw him on the night of his passing. The hand of death was already on him, but his whispered words were all of peace. He was confident we would win.

With Manny Shinwell I was very friendly despite our opposite views on defence. I was pleased to take part in the TV film of his life. His energy and vigour were astonishing. I was amazed to learn that he awoke at four each morning and read philosophy for an hour, Bertrand Russell being his favourite. One had not suspected that. Manny and I were often in different camps politically, but I always admired his loyalty to his convictions.

I suppose Mrs Thatcher must be described as a Creator of Our Time. I regard it as a bad time, strengthening competitiveness in society instead of co-operation, but circumstances led us into friendly association. She lived near me in Finchley and on late nights would drive me home from the Commons. I remember one night she asked me what I had wanted to be. I replied I had never thought about it – I only wanted to *do*. 'But to do you must be,' she protested. I hate fundamentally nearly all that Mrs Thatcher has done as Prime Minister, but I acknowledge her dedication to her convictions. She believes in capitalism and has applied her beliefs. I wish many Labour spokesmen believed in Socialism as completely.

I have left to the last Leslie Hale, later Lord Hale, because with him I had the longest comradeship. I knew Leslie for long periods, both in the Commons and the Lords. He was a brilliant parliamentarian, a challenge to the shorthand writer by his speed of speech. Why he was not made a minister is a mystery. Unfortunately, he died in November 1984. I write more fully about him in a chapter on 'Happenings'.

Many of the most effective creators of our time have been leaders of movements in colonial territories for independence. I have been associated with most of them and write of them later. I think the greatest privilege of my life was my association with Mahatma Gandhi. About him, too, I write in a later chapter.

2

The Lords: An Alternative

I have been amazingly lucky at every stage of my life in having the opportunity to do the job which expressed my convictions. The one doubt has been in these later years my membership of the House of Lords.

When I was an orthodox Christian I was a junior on the *Examiner*, the organ of the Congregationalists. When I rejected the supernatural in Jesus I became sub-editor of the *Christian Commonwealth*, the organ of R.J. Campbell's New Theology. When Socialism became my religion I was appointed editor of the *Labour Leader*, the organ of the then influential Independent Labour Party.

After my imprisonment during the First World War I felt my first duty was to expose conditions in prison, and I was invited to be joint Secretary of the Prison System Enquiry Committee. When I did research for Gandhi on Non-Co-operation I was appointed joint Secretary of the British Committee of the Indian National Congress.

During the next thirty years I held top posts in the ILP, Secretary and Chairman, and became editor of the renamed *New Leader*, followed by fifteen years in the House of Commons and more than twenty in the House of Lords. All of this enabled me to campaign for what I believe in most:

democratic Socialism, colonial liberation, human rights, disarmament and peace. There can be few who have had this good fortune of always doing what they wanted to do.

In earlier books I have covered most of my life. Here I begin with my joining the Lords. I was defeated in 1964 at Eton and Slough by eleven votes, partly on the colour issue, more so by poor organization. Strangely, it was Tony Benn, who had made history by refusing to enter the House of Lords, who first urged me to become a peer. He cited the radical stand of his father in the Upper Chamber and I remembered having seen him in action. When Harold Wilson, now himself a Lord, asked me to go to the Lords I said I didn't believe in the place but was prepared to use it as a platform. That I tried for many years to do, putting more questions, initiating more debates and introducing more Bills than any other back-bencher.

My first surprise in the House of Lords was to find that it is conducted like a Quaker meeting. I had assumed that the Lord Chancellor, wigged and gowned on the Woolsack, would control proceedings like the Speaker does in the Commons. But no, he only announces business and, curiously stepping to one side, answers questions as a minister and takes part in debates. During Committee stages of Bills, he even speaks from the front bench. We have no Chairman to keep us in order. Exactly like the Quakers with their Elders, we have a Leader of the House who gently rises to suggest that, if it be the will of the House, we should proceed to the next business. The system works admirably. The ironic fact is that it is the House of Commons which looks like a Quaker meeting-place, while the House of Lords looks like a cathedral.

One can easily be psychologically seduced in the Lords. The place is so friendly; before long everyone called me 'Fenner'. In the Bishops' Bar (so called not because the noble prelates like a tot, though most of them do, but because it was once their dressing-room), hardened Tories, even ministers, insist on sharing drinks and chat at tables over coffee. Political differences do not matter. Enjoying the privileges of the best club in London, we are equals, whatever the differences in our lives outside. There is the danger that this camaraderie might lessen one's dedication to political principles. Even in the proceedings of the House we are ostentatiously polite to each other. There is little of the bitterness between parties which occurs in the Commons.

For nearly twenty years it was difficult to recognize the leadership of the Labour Party in the Lords as Socialist. There were a few on the front bench who were outspoken, but it was not until the extended creation of life peers that vigour was added both to the front and back benches. I admit the climate of the House has affected me. I have expressed my Socialist and internationalist principles forthrightly - indeed more than one member of the party has called me its conscience - but I have done so without the belligerence which had been mine in the Commons. Is this a surrender?

The absence of dominating partisanship probably adds to the effectiveness of debates; mostly they are quietly argued and appeal to reason. They are often better than in the Commons. This is for two additional reasons. We have a number of exceptionally informed members of the House, appointed for their experience in the civil, colonial and foreign services, in the professions, as judges, as academics, as ex-ministers. Their speeches are almost invariably worth listening to, not only for their knowledge but for their analysis and mature judgement. In the earlier years debates on social issues were not so good because most peers had little knowledge of working-class conditions, but the increase in Labour life peers went some way towards correcting this. The second reason is that one knows that most speakers are expressing the truth as they see it. The House of Lords is much freer than the Commons from pressure to toe the party line. The exceptions are a few Lords who seek promotion and members of the front benches who have to express the official view of the Government or Opposition. I have heard, for instance, a minister rather pathetically defending a Bill which he had voted against as a back-bencher. Such instances are few. Most debates reflect both sincerity and knowledge. I doubt whether the standard is higher in any legislature in the world.

Question Time is not so exciting as in the Commons, but I think most of those who have listened to both from the public galleries would agree that it is more impressive. Our procedure is different. Only four questions a day are permitted on the Order Paper, which means that each can be explored in some depth. In fact, there is often a minor debate because views can be expressed by the device of asking the minister if he or she is aware of so and so. For some years I used to table questions nearly every day, so much so that a Tory asked how much my questions cost. Then three new life peers, Lords Jenkins of Putney, Hatch of Lusby and Bill Molloy, also put down so many questions that a rule was introduced limiting them severely. Many more Lords are now tabling questions. The chamber is full for the allotted half-hour.

A great change has taken place in the activity of the Lords. When I joined the House, back-benchers were not expected to work. There were two small rooms on the ground floor with four desks in each for Government and Opposition Lords. I occupied a large desk which had previously been used by Earl Attlee. Even ex-Prime Ministers had limited accommodation for their work. Ritchie Calder, a memorable friend, had another desk. Now there are desks with telephones for about fifty backbenchers and there is keen competition for vacancies. Conditions are still unsatisfactory. Although the attendance allowance includes an item for secretarial assistance, there is nowhere in the House where secretaries can work.

A word about the daily allowance. Members of the House receive no salary but can claim an allowance for expenses when they attend. The full allowances were, in 1985, £36 per day, £18 per day being for secretarial expenses. In one recent parliamentary year the Lords met 178 days, so the total amount which could be claimed (apart from travel to and from the House) was £6,408. This was supposed to cover expenses only; the cost of meals, drinks and entertainment of visitors is also heavy. But undoubtedly the payment for attendance is responsible for the presence of many. Even so, I would put the average attendance at less than 300 of the one thousand members.

I have been deeply impressed both at Question Time and during debates by the quality of the homework done by those on the front benches. They appear almost invariably masters of their subjects in detail. This is largely due to the skilled help of the civil servants and of the Opposition research workers. At first I was amazed how ministers could nearly always read from a brief replies to the Supplementary Questions. The civil servants with remarkable thoroughness had foreseen what would be asked. I was baffled by this anticipation when I put questions. But ministers and Opposition spokespersons themselves obviously spend hours studying their parts, particularly during the Committee stages of complicated Bills. They get little recognition. The newspapers give scant attention to what happens in the Lords:

it is ministers in the House of Commons who make reputations.

I was in favour of televising the House of Lords because I believe the public has a right to know what happens in Parliament, but I unhappily recognized that it would make the Lords more popular. Nevertheless, I hope the House of Commons will follow our example.

During my time in the Lords we have had both Labour and Conservative Governments. My criticism of the Labour Governments was about their policies on immigration, arms expenditure and Northern Ireland, and about their failure to apply Socialist remedies for homelessness and unemployment. I nearly defeated the Government once. In their 1971 Immigration Act they refused permission of entry into this country to Indian holders of British passports in Kenya. Leading Tories, who had been party to an undertaking that those who opted for British citizenship would enjoy its privileges, indicated that they would vote for my motion to reject the Bill. It looked as though I might win. Eddie Shackleton, who was leading for the Government, met me outside the Chamber to discuss an accommodation. We were still talking when the Chief Whip arrived to assure him that the Bill would get through. It was carried by a small majority.

I introduced three Bills in the House of Lords. The first was to extend the Racial Discrimination Act. In the Commons I had introduced a Bill nine years in succession against racial discrimination. At first it was comprehensive, but to have a hope of success I limited the ninth edition to discrimination in public places. The Labour Government adopted and enacted this. But experience showed that it failed to deal with the two worst spheres of discrimination: homes and jobs. It was in November 1966 that I introduced in the Lords a Bill to amend the Racial Discrimination Act further. The purpose was to extend it to both racial and religious discrimination in places of public resort, employment and housing. I added religious discrimination because of the many faiths in Britain and because I hoped it would be an example for Northern Ireland, which unfortunately the Bill did not cover.

The Labour front bench opposed it on the grounds that the Government was considering an amending Bill but had not completed its discussions, and the Bill was defeated. Later the Government did introduce a Bill dealing with employment and housing, though it did not include religious discrimination. It has had some effect. Local authorities in general have accepted it in allotting houses, and the largest industrial companies have applied it. But colour discrimination persists, with disastrous consequences among school-leavers. The high percentage of young blacks who cannot get a job is creating a dangerous anti-society psychology.

The two other Bills were in favour of civil rights in Northern Ireland. I took the view that if Stormont were required to apply a code of civil rights this would be a greater permanent guarantee of stability than power-sharing. A coalition of Protestants, largely capitalist-led, and of Catholics, tending to radicalism, would result in an indecisive government doing little. I got considerable support for these Bills, but the civil-rights movement in Northern Ireland lost strength to extremism. I was at the watershed. I was in Londonderry, addressing a legal civil-rights demonstration on Bloody Sunday, when scores of unarmed and fleeing Irish were shot after some stone-throwing. I gave evidence at the official enquiry, but the only thing I said that was reproduced in the report was that the British soldiers had not directed their shots at our meeting – a whitewash report.

During my time in the Lords there have been about a dozen members who might be described as belonging to the Left. I am pleased to have been associated with them in urging radical domestic and foreign policies. I think particularly of Bruce of Donington, who makes challenging contributions from the front bench; Ritchie Calder and Wynne-Jones, so effectively using their knowledge; Hugh Jenkins of Putney, who is persistent in opposing nuclear weapons; John Hatch of Lusby, particularly informed on Africa; Wedderburn, of the London School of Economics, a specialist in industrial law; Leslie Hale, my comrade at home and in Africa over many years; Tony Gifford, barrister, always ready to defend dissidents; Bill Molloy, devastating in his criticism of the cuts in the Health Service; Donald Soper, as outspoken for pacifism in the Lords as on Tower Hill. There are a number of others. They will forgive me for not mentioning them, but where shall I stop?

Most of all, while he lived, I co-operated with Philip Noel-Baker. Together we established the World Disarmament Campaign (UK). He had been appointed by the Labour Government to the British team at the first UN Special Session on Disarmament in 1978 and was enthusiastic about its recommendations for the early destruction of nuclear weapons, the phased abolition of conventional weapons, general and complete disarmament, and the transference of military expenditure to development, with the aim of ending world poverty. We decided to initiate a world campaign to realize these objects. I describe its progress later; here I will refer only to our co-operation in the Lords. Philip was nearly blind and somewhat deaf. He was not able to participate in the exchange following questions which I put, but opportunities arose often in debates. Philip's speeches were amazing. He revealed an astonishing memory for facts and dates and developed his argument with a passion and rhetoric which held the House silent. Even those who disagreed recognized that his was the voice of humanity.

There are women in the House. They prove how absurd is the view that women are not equal to men in politics. Both front benches have able women and among back-benchers they are prominent. After all, they have been made life peers for outstanding public service.

In recent years I have done comparatively little in the House. I have almost joined the silent majority. Occasionally I intervene in the exchanges at Question Time. Very rarely do I speak in debates. This is due to two things. First, I have become increasingly deaf. My hearing-aid does not let me follow what is being said and other devices leave me frustrated. This limits severely my participation in exchanges in the House. Second, I have devoted myself so entirely to the cause of disarmament that I have dropped my interest, or rather activity, in other subjects. Earlier I had informed myself on most humanitarian issues; human rights, racial equality, apartheid, Namibia, the Brandt reports, the law of the sea, the Palestinians, the multinational companies and other international subjects. Now I concentrate so much on disarmament that I leave this broad scope to others.

It may be that my limited opportunity for activity has led to an increasing doubt as to whether I was right to accept the invitation to become a Lord. I have always disliked being called a Lord. I hate elitism and the term denotes superior status. My wife holds this view so strongly that she refuses to be called Lady Brockway. Also, while I had agreed to join the Lords in order to use it as a platform, experience shows that it is a poor platform. Rarely are one's remarks reported. I have begun to feel that I would have served better the causes to which I am devoted by giving my services to the remarkable pressure movements which have developed in the last twenty years - CND, the National Council for Civil Liberties, Liberation (successor to the Movement for Colonial Freedom), the British section of Amnesty International, Shelter, the World Disarmament Campaign and others. I felt this particularly after the World Disarmament Campaign was formed. I addressed crowded meetings, often two a week, and found that I was providing welcome information to the already converted and that I was making new converts. Often I had standing ovations, though these were probably for my age rather than my words. Moreover, free from my duties in the Lords, I could give more time to administrative work and to world contacts, and I could do more writing. I remain doubtful as to whether I was right to enter the Lords.

I have never hidden my view that the House of Lords should be abolished as a legislative Chamber. In 1982, to my surprise, I carried a motion at the not progressive Oxford Union in favour of its abolition, despite opposition from a Minister, Lord Gowrie, and Lord Shackleton, who had been the Labour Party Leader. Eric Heffer seconded me. The present composition of the Lords is ludicrous in a democratic society. Nearly eight hundred of the one thousand or so members are hereditary peers: the Labour Opposition is in a permanent minority.

The difficulty is that if the membership were democratized the House of Lords would become a rival to the House of Commons. For example, the proposal that a Second Chamber should be elected by proportional representation would certainly lead to the claim that it was more representative than

Membership of House of Lords (June 1985)	
Hereditary peers	792
Life peers	365
Archbishops and bishops	26
Women members	66
Conservative	413
Cross-bench	230
Labour	127
Liberal	42
Social Democrat	44
Number of members	1183

the Commons. Similarly, the suggestion that it should be elected by the local authorities would bring about the claim that the Lords were more in touch with the grassroots than members of the Commons. The argument that the Lords are of value as a revising Chamber is largely disproved in practice. It is disproved often when the Lords carry an amendment to a Bill against the wishes of the Government. If on going back to the Commons the amendment is rejected, the Lords submit.

The function of revision could certainly be undertaken by other means. The procedure of the House of Commons would require to be drastically altered if the powers of the House of Lords were abolished. The need for some revising body is clear. This could be met by the appointment of a highly qualified representative Select Committee which would have the power to propose amendments to the full House before the Bill became law. This would also enable the Government to propose second-thought amendments which are sometimes introduced in the Lords.

While abolishing a Second Chamber with legislative powers I would retain a Second Chamber with important consultative powers. Of whom should it be composed and what should be the scope of its functions? I suggest that an effective consultative Chamber should include five groups. They would represent the composition of the nation, its mind and its activities.

First, a group of nominated members valued for their knowledge. I have already written that debates are often better in the Lords than in the Commons and that this is because life peers contribute from their experience in many spheres of life. Members of the Commons sometimes describe the Lords as the House of Geriatrics, but there is something to be said for the mature advice of the elderly in the making of law. In Africa, the tribal communities were ruled effectively by respected elders.

The second group should consist of representatives from selected regional and local authorities. This would allow members of the comprehensive structure of the democratic constitution of the country to voice their opinions on proposed legislation as it affected them. It would valuably coordinate the strands of democratic Britain.

Third, industrial and working people, the CBI and the TUC, the boards of directors of the nationalized industries and of the leading private industries, together with the trade unions within them, should be represented. Agriculture could be represented by the National Farmers Union and the agricultural workers' section of the TGWU. We must not forget the public services, the National Health Service, Education and Transport: both the managements and the workers must have a voice. The Civil Service must also be included in the Chamber.

Fourth, the nation's womanhood, through representatives appointed by the women's organizations, occupational, political and cultural should be heard. This would compensate a little for the under-representation of women in the Commons.

A method must be found of representing housewives, who are without an organization.

Lastly, I propose representation of the main grassroots non-governmental pressure organizations in the country. This was first suggested to me by Joan Hymans. It has a precedent in the non-governmental organizations of the United Nations. Representation of such groups in a consultative Chamber would mean that the voice of the most politically alert and active of our citizens could be directly heard in our Parliament; the champions of the homeless, of child poverty and peace. It would make the Chamber a democratic assembly. Often, as in the case of the Welfare Societies, such as Oxfam, and the British Medical Association, it would contribute expert knowledge for consideration.

The functions of the consultative Chamber might be similar to those of the non-governmental organizations associated with the United Nations. Their documents would be distributed to all Members of Parliament. They would be permitted to give evidence to Select Committees of the Commons and even on special occasions to address the Commons from the Bar of the House. They would debate every legislative issue and their speeches would be recorded in Hansard. Because of the uniquely democratic constitution of the Chamber, the media might give its debates more notice than they give the House of Lords.

The method of appointment to membership of the consultative Chamber might be as follows. The group of experienced elders should be nominated by a very representative Select Committee of the Commons, which should also select the regional and local authorities, and the series of organizations which I have cited in the different categories. Then these should appoint their members.

These suggestions are not made dogmatically,

and other means may be thought out, but I believe there is undoubtedly a case for a representative consultative Chamber which could maintain democratic contact between the dynamic organizations of the people and Parliament and Government during their five-year rule. To have their representatives at Westminster ready for consultation would itself be administratively valuable. To provide them with an organ for the expression of their views, whenever relevant to decisions to be made by Parliament, would expand electoral democracy, adding community democracy, and making the influence of the people continuously alive. Is not the proposal worth consideration?

3

An Unfinished Revolution

I am an optimist because I have seen accomplished three great changes in our society. Those who urged these changes at the beginning of this century were dismissed as lonely and impossible voices. The first is the Welfare State, established by the Labour Government elected in 1945.

In my first public speech at an ILP demonstration in 1907 outside Finsbury Town Hall, I called for benefits for the unemployed. I lived at a settlement in an Islington slum where poverty was so great that the majority of families were hungry. The only provision for the unemployed was the workhouse.

It was then that the campaign for the Welfare State began - not only benefits for the unemployed, but for old-age pensions, allowances for the sick and disabled, and for the feeding of hungry schoolchildren. The first achievement was meals at school. It must have been about 1908. I remember how it transformed the health of the children. Then after the 1910 elections Lloyd George introduced measures which accepted the principle of a Welfare State: benefits for the unemployed and pensions for the aged. The amounts were pitifully low, but here was the beginning.

Our campaigning after that was for lifting benefits and pensions and resisting the cuts imposed under the MacDonald Government of 1929, and the National Government which followed. It was not until the Labour victory in 1945 that the Welfare State was fully established - not only benefits of a living standard for the unemployed, the sick, disabled, widows, and aged, as well as child benefits and generous school meals, but Nye Bevan's glorious National Health Service, establishing free treatment for all in need. That was the achievement of the claims we had begun to voice tentatively forty years before. How grateful we were!

The Welfare State was not a Socialist revolution but it was a social revolution. It ended starvation in Britain. It was an unfinished revolution which still needs to be completed by the transformation of the basis of society itself.

The Labour Government elected in 1945 was more Socialist than any in Britain before or since. It not only established the Welfare State but took into public ownership mines, railways and steel. Its great failure was to begin disastrous rearmament. There was controversy between Herbert Morrison and Nye Bevan over the form of nationalization. Morrison established the corporations, independent of parliamentary control. Bevan wanted administration responsible to Parliament. I don't think either expressed the fundamental issue. The real failure of Morrison's plan was the absence of industrial democracy, workers' participation in management.

We all regarded nationalization as a great Socialist advance. At Merthyr Tydfil the railway workers attached posters to the trucks, 'These are ours now.' No railway worker feels that today. No miner feels that the pits are his. No steelworker felt that the industrial plant was his.

We have had strikes in all three nationalized industries, the most impressive being the miners' strike of 1984. The reason is that there has been no democratic control within the industries. Governments have appointed chairmen and board members to run the industries at huge salaries without accountability to the workers.

The most notorious example was Mr (now Sir) Ian MacGregor, the Chairman of the NCB, an American tycoon, who was given the colossal salary of £59,325 a year. An American firm, of which he was a director, was paid £1 million to release him. As though any man is such a superperson! He decided to close down pits without any agreement with the workers. It has become abundantly clear that the nationalization of the mines was not Socialism.

Nye Bevan's plea for parliamentary control might have improved matters, but with varying consequences as Labour and Conservative administrations alternated in authority. The real Socialist solution was what was termed 'workers' control', the representation of workers on the controlling boards, from local management to national control. This would have been industrial democracy.

In fact, Manny Shinwell, who, as Minister of Fuel, was responsible for nationalizing the mines, offered the miners a beginning of industrial democracy. He asked the unions to appoint three members of the National Coal Board. Whether that was an adequate number for a real share in management could be doubted, but he had the right idea. 'I want you to regard yourselves in the future not as employees but as partners,' he said. That surely is the essence of democratic Socialism – a partnership of workers and the community. But the miners' union under the leadership of Sir William Lawther refused: they were concerned not with control but with winning wage increases, shorter hours and safer conditions from those who *did* control. There was no conception of the constructive functions of trade unions in a new co-operative social order.

We call ourselves a democracy. We have an elected Parliament and elected local authorities. But the real rulers of the country are the boards of management of our industries. The Inland Revenue Statistics, 1984, showed that 1% of the adult population of Britain owned 21% of the marketable wealth in 1982; that 5% owned 41%, that 10% owned 56% and that half owned 96%. The nationalized industries help to maintain this imbalance by the high salaries of their appointed chairmen and directors, compared with the wages of the workers. The only protection for the worker is the pressure of the trade unions, whose authority in negotiation was minimized in the eighties by high unemployment. Within the nationalized industries the class structure persists. It is as much a division between managers and workers, between 'us' and 'them', as it is in private industry.

'Us' and 'them' is the fundamental division in our community. It was increased by the confrontational nature of Mrs Thatcher's rule in the 1980s. It exists in all industry and spreads over into most social relations. It is an inevitable accompaniment to the capitalist system. The Liberals advocate industrial democracy within privately owned industries. That would be a temporary advance, but it would identify the workers with their own company against others. It would divide the workers and would retain the system of competition rather than co-operation. The Socialist plan for workers' control, for industrial democracy, must be based on public ownership, expressing the motive that production and services are directly for the community and not for the profit of private owners.

The actual method of applying industrial

democracy would have to be worked out. It might be that on the central controlling authority there would be 40% representation of the workers and 40% of the management (representing, it is to be hoped, extended public ownership), with 20% representation of other industries served and the consuming public. On issues concerning working conditions, the controlling authority might be 50% each of workers' representatives and management. These suggestions are not dogmatic. The plan would have to be agreed between the Government, the TUC and, as long as private ownership persists, the CBI. The purpose would be to end the psychology of 'us' and 'them', to encourage workers to feel that the plants in which they work are theirs, preferably in partnership with the community. When that comes about, the prevalence of strikes will be over.

Industrial democracy would do much to identify the people, men and women in everyday life, with publicly owned enterprises. The centralization of these industries makes their administration so distant, so out of reach, so impossible to influence, that the mass of people has lost interest in what goes on. The public to whom the industries are supposed to belong is indifferent. Publicly distributed information would be one answer, but the involvement of workers and consumers in management would have the greatest effect in spreading the feeling that the industries were 'ours'. There is also a case for devolving central control. A representative commission should examine possibilities. Small is not only beautiful; in the case of localized management it is an important basis of democratic participation.

It is impossible to describe the series of Labour Governments which we have had since 1950 as

Socialist. They did little for the transformation of society. The recession came. Surely this should have been seized upon as evidence of the failure of the capitalist system itself? Not only were workers unemployed, but plants were idle. This was because there was no demand for their products; the mass of the people had not the necessary purchasing power, due to the unequal distribution of wealth. There were, of course, other elements, such as oil prices, high interest rates, the fluctuation of currency values and so on, but the fundamental cause was the inability of the people, including those in the Third World, to make a demand for goods. I do not say that the recession meant the collapse of capitalism. Since the nineteenth century there have been repeated recessions involving extensive unemployment, most worse than their predecessors in depth and length. Capitalism recovers. The time comes when stocks of goods are at last purchased and restoration begins.

Surprisingly, Mrs Thatcher succeeded in the recession of the eighties in maintaining her control, despite more than three million unemployed and an untold number of bankruptcies. She has proudly defended her capitalist system, using her majority in Parliament not only to undermine the Welfare State but to sell to private purchasers publicly owned enterprises. Mrs Thatcher explained the Government's inability to do more to end the recession by saying it was worldwide. Of course it was. Capitalism was worldwide except for the Communist countries, which also, though to a lesser extent, felt its effects. In the countries of the West we have 36 million unemployed. The situation is ironical. Technical advance has enabled the world's industry, if fully used, to end poverty in the world within a decade. I repeat: it is not being used because the people have not the wherewithal to purchase its potential products. The recession was due to the unequal wealth distribution inherent in the capitalist system.

I have written that I wish the Labour leadership showed the same enthusiasm for Socialism as Mrs Thatcher shows for capitalism. In the early eighties there was a tremendous opportunity. Capitalism worldwide was failing. A Socialist transformation was the only way in which the situation could be changed and the millions of unemployed provided with work and honourable income. Labour spokespersons failed to argue this. They did not demand Socialism, but addressed failures within capitalism.

An international Socialist plan was required. Willy Brandt was the Chairman of the Socialist International. In 1983 he was instrumental in producing a report to save the Third World from poverty – 'The Report of the Independent Commission on International Development Issues'. Why did not all the Socialist parties get together to plan an international Socialist transformation, revolutionary but constructive and realistic, making the decisive break with capitalism? The situation pleaded for it. Instead, Socialists in each country, Britain included, forgetting their internationalism, began to urge the restriction of imports to protect their own unemployed – i.e. protection by making workers in other countries unemployed. Restriction of imports is justified when International Labour Organization conditions are breached. Some international agreement should be reached on state subsidies. But to prevent imports generally is a denial of Socialist internationalism.

A great opportunity was missed. Capitalism was obviously failing. Do we believe that democratic Socialism is the answer? Then why don't we plan it and make it the political issue of our time?

Every member of the Labour Party has signed the membership form which selects this clause from its constitution as its basic objective:

> To secure for the workers by hand or by brain the full fruits of their industry and the most equitable distribution thereof that may be possible upon the basis of the common ownership of the means of production, distribution and exchange, and the best obtainable system of popular administration and control of each industry or service.

But how many accept it seriously? The impression is given in parliamentary debates and speeches in the country that the party's objective is reform within capitalism. The public is given no picture of the new social order which is our stated aim. The party is described as Socialist with the consequence that, because its spokespersons concern themselves only with immediate reforms, the public has no idea of our fundamental objective. We need above everything an organization within the Labour Party which, like the ILP used to do, devotes itself entirely to education in the basic transformation which Socialism means, and which advocates policies to realize it.

The Labour Party brought about its own defeat in the General Election of 1983. All the cards were in its hands. No Government in modern times had such a record of failure as Mrs Thatcher's. Labour's defeat was blamed on the leadership of Michael Foot. That was only partly true. Michael was splendid. He was tireless and his speeches to vast crowds were inspiring. But on television - and this was determining - he did not win confidence as a potential Prime Minister. A wonderful propagandist, but not a statesman.

The cause of defeat, however, was not Michael's personality. There were - or should have been - two supreme issues, unemployment and peace. The party had prepared a detailed policy statement on unemployment, but it failed to get it across in simple human terms. The country needs thousands of homes; millions of people are living in overcrowded and insanitary conditions and many are even homeless. We need hospitals, as the long waiting-lists prove. We need many modern schools. Break into unemployment by providing these needs! As for peace and nuclear disarmament, the different views expressed by the Labour leaders caused profound doubts and cynicism. It was confusion about what a Labour Government would do which lost votes.

The election showed how unfair our electoral system is. In 1983 the Conservatives polled 42.4% of the total votes and returned 397 MPs. The Labour Party polled 27.6% and returned 209. But the Liberal-Social Democratic Alliance polled 25.4% and returned only twenty-three MPs. Mrs Thatcher's Government reflected less than half of the vote. Similar disproportions were shown in the election for the European Parliament in 1984.

We cannot call Britain a political democracy while the present electoral system continues. The Labour Party opposes proportional representation because experience proves that it leads to unstable government with many parties, and without any party having a majority. The consequence is weak coalition government. I will return to that in a moment, but the fundamental question is - do we sincerely believe in democracy? If so, we surely must be in favour of a Parliament which reflects public opinion. That means that we should have some system of proportional representation.

Democracy requires not only a true reflection of public opinion, but contact between the electors and the elected. Only thus can members of a legislature continually reflect public opinion. The most accurate reflection of opinion would be one nationwide poll - lists of nominees in order of preference prepared by the political parties - but democratic contact would then be impossible. Some advocates of proportional representation propose constituencies with six members. Even that would make close association between a Member of Parliament and his or her constituents impossible. I therefore favour single-member constituencies with a transferable vote (the second preference of those who voted for the bottom candidate being transferred to the candidates above him or her), or alternatively, a second ballot when no candidate obtains an overall majority.

The argument that proportional representation involves unstable and weak government is formidable. Much of Europe illustrates it. For Socialists, this is particularly frustrating. I would argue, however, that if we are *democratic* Socialists we cannot wish to make our transformation of society until we have the majority of the people behind us. Indeed, the task is so great that for certainty we should need such support. Otherwise the change could be made only by a dictatorship. That leaves, however, the question of instability of government unanswered. I believe a proposal made by the ILP in the twenties provides the clue. Under proportional representation Labour would at some point be returned as the largest party. Its leader would then be called upon to form a government. Let the leader establish not a coalition but a minority Government. The ILP proposed that such a government should first introduce urgently needed and popular reforms, such as (today) living benefits, the reconstruction of the National Health Service, and a big housing programme, and after that decisive Socialist measures. On these it would invite defeat, but in the succeeding election Socialism would be the issue. That proposal is relevant not only to conditions under proportional representation. Many of us urged it on the minority

Labour Governments of 1924 and 1929. We would have liked to have seen it adopted by the minority Governments in the seventies. Socialism would have then become alive. As it is, even within the Labour Party, it is regarded as a distant goal irrelevant to immediate issues.

The ILP in the twenties, under the constructive leadership of Clifford Allen, had bright ideas. It appointed an influential committee to prepare proposals for 'Socialism in Our Time'. Its members included J.A. Hobson, authoritative in economics, and H.N. Brailsford, authoritative in so many spheres. Their report is extraordinarily appropriate today.

Starvation has been ended in Britain by the Welfare State, but many thousands of people still live below a human level. The ILP report proposed the establishment of a living income level for all, not only in the benefit paid to the disabled and unemployed and in the pensions paid to the aged, but as a compulsory minimum for all wage-earners. Thus poverty would be ended. I was encouraged by the decision of the Trades Union Congress in 1985 in favour of a national minimum wage. The General Council is to report whether it should be achieved by statute and be legally enforceable, or by collective bargaining. The Congress agreed that it would hold 'without prejudice' discussions on a statutory minimum wage with any future sympathetic Government. This represents a great advance.

Personally, I take the view of Bernard Shaw that Socialism should involve equality of incomes for all. It is unjust that higher incomes should be received by those whose work is done in the most comfortable conditions and that the lowest wages should go to those whose conditions are harshest. I appreciate, however, that such equality, which would demand a new social ethic, is far off.

Meanwhile, one hopes that the Labour Party will adopt the proposal for a compulsory living income for all. The ILP report also proposed the public ownership of financial institutions and the key industries. Any Socialist programme would of course have to include this, accompanied by the industrial democracy I have already described.

It is at present widely rejected, but a Socialist Government must have an incomes policy. The Labour Party emphasizes its purpose of redistributing wealth, but its present means of doing so are pathetically inadequate. It would use taxation, increasing demands on the rich and decreasing them on the less well-off. Labour would also extend public services and so lift social incomes. But that would leave untouched the gross inequality of wealth distribution. I have already described how in 1984 5% of the adult population owned 41% of the marketable wealth. Every week newspapers describe high salary increases to managements already receiving many thousands of pounds annually. One of such repeated reports caught my eye in November 1984. It recorded that the Chairman of the Burton Group, the fashion retailers, Ralph Halpern, had his annual salary increased from £199,000 to £348,000, including bonuses. The other directors also benefited. Their bonuses were pushed up from £355,000 to £877,000 and their salaries were increased from £634,000 to £802,000. Mr Halpern defended the increases by saying it was important to 'motivate' people who were running the company. Running the company! What of all the sub-managers and the shop-floor workers? One was not told whether their incomes were increased. Shop-floor workers are not generally the best paid. And compare for a moment these salaries of hundreds of thousands of pounds with the average annual income of £9,300 for men and £6,000 for women in 1984. Can one begin to justify such wealth distribution?

Labour's incomes policy should include a maximum salary as well as a minimum wage. It is said that this would mean that those who had received above the maximum salary would emigrate and take jobs where salaries were unlimited. So much for their patriotism! But are not the individual abilities of those with high salaries often exaggerated? Is success really due to them? If they resigned, would not many who assist them be capable of taking over their posts?

In 1985 the Trade Union Movement opposed the adoption of an incomes policy by a Labour Government. It claimed that determination of incomes is exclusively its own province in negotiation with employers. The unions once opposed child benefits on the ground that they affected the family wage. They adjusted their attitude as they realized the benefit the community would receive. The mood of trade unionism is still largely that of a dissident organization within capitalism. It is only beginning to think in terms of a constructive function in a transformed society. If we had a Socialist Government seriously engaged in making that transformation, trade unions might be expected to adjust their attitude. They would become consciously a co-operative part of that transformation. They could surely be counted upon to become active participants in wealth redistribution.

Mrs Thatcher won the election in 1983 largely because she emphasized the importance of individual opportunity and satisfaction. She stood for a society in which effort and possession were dominant over dependence on aid from the Government or public authorities. She reflected this in her decision to allow the tenants of publicly owned housing estates to buy their houses. The Labour Party, nationally and locally, opposed this move on the grounds that it would undermine the principle of public ownership, the provision of houses for those most in need. But home-ownership is a natural desire of many families. The home is the intimate focus of parental love, of the rearing of children, of giving hospitality to friends.

I think the Labour Party was wrong to oppose the sale on principle. The conditions of sale were a different matter. Purchasers should not have been bribed to buy by low prices. The principle of the provision of houses for those in need should have been retained by insistence that if the owner wished later to sell the house it should be returned to the public authority at the price he or she paid for it plus an allowance for inflation. Thus the motive of profit-making would have been avoided.

Socialists have been inclined to exaggerate the importance of collectivism over individualism. After all, our object is to provide every individual who is born with the opportunity to reach fulfilment physically, mentally and spiritually. Collectivism should be the platform for such development. The aim should be the development of the individual.

The tendency to emphasize collectivism has been shown in the conviction that aid to an individual in need should come only through public authorities. Help given by private agencies has been regarded as charity. But democracy in a community cannot depend only on what elected authorities do. Democracy means that the people themselves should be inspired to perform social services, to become themselves associated in endeavours to make their communities just, co-operative and beautiful. Local community bodies should be encouraged in the same way as national non-governmental bodies. The early Co-operative Movement was a splendid effort by the people themselves.

I have done some research into community activities and am amazed at their number and variety. In every locality they seem to cover all aspects of life. Most of them are concerned in assisting those who have difficulties in their lives; others are co-operative in common occupations and hobbies, seeking to serve the development of their communities. For example, I have a list of ninety societies embracing every sort of social activity within one local community. Admittedly some of the associations are reactionary, but better committed opposition than indifference. From the clash of opinions comes truth. This is democracy at grassroots. It involves groups of volunteers becoming active in service, helping those in need, combining to make the environment better. A creative democracy would defend not only activity by elected authorities but at the roots; co-operation by the people themselves. Only thus would we have a vital democratic Socialism.

In the beginning Socialism was a human crusade, its adherents passionately concerned to end the poverty which deformed lives, to create a society of co-operation and fellowship among equals, expressing the ethic of community service rather than individual aggrandisement. Today that human passion has been largely lost. The Labour Party has tended to become a political contender for power, concerned about current issues within capitalism rather than a transformation of the basis of society. Many supporters of the Labour Party, even many members, are not Socialists at all. Their interests are in issues which arise in Parliament which do not begin to suggest a transformation of society. I repeat that we need today within the Labour Party an educational body which will ceaselessly spread the fundamental principles of Socialism as the ILP did in its better days. Happily there is still in party membership a host of comrades to whom Socialism is a human crusade, and who cling to its basic principles.

I began by emphasizing the importance of internationalism. If we had the spirit of internationalism we should seek to end poverty not only in Britain but in the world. I shall be dealing with the problem of hunger in the Third World later, but how many of us are actively concerned by the appalling fact that thirty million people die every year from starvation or medical neglect? If Socialism were a human crusade, that could never be forgotten.

I have been critical and pessimistic, but I am still an optimist. In the eighties there was a revival of real Socialism in the British Labour Movement. It was expressed at first in the speeches and activity of Tony Benn and his popularity in the Party, although I differed with him later. It was reflected in the splendid radicalism of a number of elected regional and local authorities, the Greater London Council, Sheffield, Liverpool and Manchester among them. The election of Neil Kinnock as leader indicated a renewal of acceptance of radical policies, even though he disappointed me later when he appeared to become subject to the influence of the traditional majority in his shadow Cabinet. I am hopeful that by the time this book is published the Labour Party will have recovered the inspiration of earlier days.

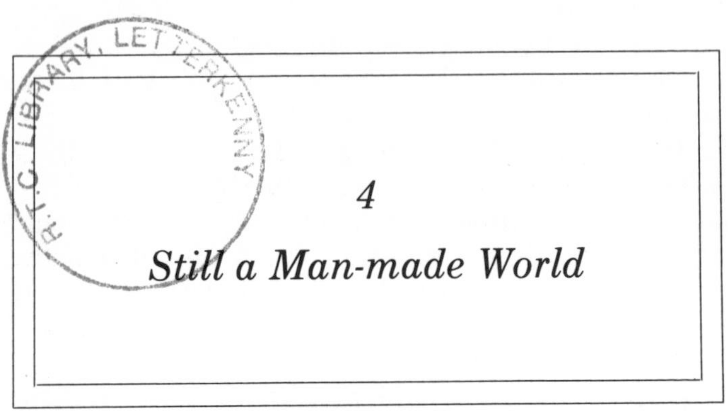

4
Still a Man-made World

The second great change which I have seen in Britain is the degree to which women have won political equality. It is difficult to realize how bitter was the opposition to votes for women at the beginning of this century. In 1908 there was a great women's suffrage demonstration in Hyde Park. The audience of half a million people included a considerable contingent of male opponents. I was there - indeed I did a little to help the Pethick-Lawrences organize it from their flat in Lincoln's Inn. I saw a group of ferocious men attempting to overthrow platforms, so that children had to be lifted to safety. My first girlfriend was a suffragette, but we parted when the Women's Suffrage Political Union adopted arson and violence.

It is popularly held that votes for women were won because of the service the suffragettes gave in the war. That is a myth. Women would have gained the vote if there had been no war. Catherine Marshall, of the constitutional suffragists, gained promises of support from the majority of MPs and candidates for the election which would have otherwise taken place. After the war, when the suffragists decided to support the Labour Party, I became its liaison officer with them. Although only in my twenties, I was invited to speak at a meeting in the Albert Hall and, looking like a lad, I was obstructed from getting to the platform because I was thought to be a press messenger! Limited enfranchisement came in 1918, votes on the same terms as men in 1928. Equality in votes had been won, but in the years which have followed there has been no political equality.

In the seventies and eighties we had, astonishingly, a series of women Prime Ministers in Israel, Sri Lanka (then Ceylon), India and Britain. But they were isolated; there were few women in their Parliaments. Britain is particularly bad in this respect. The Prime Minister is the only woman in the Cabinet. In 1985 in the House of Commons, there were only twenty-eight women among 650 members, 4.3%. In the House of Lords, there were only sixty-four women among over a thousand members. In other Parliaments women were in a larger proportion. This was especially true of Scandinavia, where the figures were: Sweden: ninety-eight women in 349 (28.4%); Denmark: forty-two women in 179 (23.2%); and Finland: sixty-one women in 200 (30.5%). Sweden had six women ministers in twenty; Denmark four in twenty-one and Finland three in seventeen. Still a minority but an improvement.

In other Parliaments the proportion of women does not reach that in Scandinavia, but is much better than in Britain.

In the eighties I took part in Britain in an organization called the 300 Group, which aims at creating 300 women MPs. It not only seeks to get women adopted as candidates but trains women who wish to be MPs in technical knowledge of policies. One of its imaginative activities is to organize debates in the largest committee room at the House of Commons, with members sitting opposite each other as in Parliament. An MP acts as the Speaker. I was present on one occasion and was fascinated.

The absence of women MPs in Britain is partly due to a conservative view in many constituency parties that women candidates would be unpopular. There is no evidence of this when the women are able. The more fundamental reason is the place women have in the structure of society. This is dealt with fully later, but women in Britain, to a much greater degree than in many other countries, are limited to unskilled employment, often part-time, together with their work as housewives. Women with time to give themselves seriously to politics are almost always those in the professions and in clerical occupations. The inequality in political representation of women is a reflection of the male domination of the social structure.

I was brought up in the Victorian age when women were utterly subordinate. A few brilliant women overcame this as writers and artists, but generally women were regarded as the servants of men, both socially and physically. I wondered when Mrs Thatcher asked us to return to Victorian values whether she had thought of this. It was a hypocritical age, superficially endorsing marital fidelity, regarding sex as a dirty word, but with men widely following the Prince of Wales in his bachelor promiscuity. There was no sex education. Sex was a subject which was not talked about, at least publicly. Most boys grew up without any idea of how to satisfy women in sex. Girls grew up without knowing that they could be satisfied. It was regarded merely as an act of satisfaction for the male appetite. I may have overstated, but I write from my own experience.

Halfway through the twentieth century there was a great reaction. By the seventies and eighties we had reached the permissive society. This was largely due to the widespread use by women of contraceptives, particularly the pill, commonly adopted by girls as they became sexually mature, despite some disturbing side-effects. Sex ceased to be a dirty word. Sex education became common. The sexual act was accepted as a means to mutual satisfaction.

This was a victory for women's equality, the full consequences of which we have not yet seen. Many couples live together openly without marriage, but generally marriage is still seen as desirable when a child is to be born.

There is still a case for continuous living together by couples. Women want children, and there is nothing happier than a family where love is all around. Probably in the majority of cases that continues until the children are grown up. But the number of divorces has risen, owing not only to infidelity, even in a permissive society, but often because the man asserts himself as head of the family. There are cases where a husband objects to his wife developing outside interests, becoming involved in causes, going to meetings. The traditional view persists; she is his wife to serve him. More often than is recognized divorces occur because the woman develops a self-respect which does not accept domination. Sometimes the domination is violent. A quarter of violent crimes in the early eighties were assaults on wives. Few of the dominating husbands probably realize that they are symbolic of relationships between men and women embodied deeply in the social structure, not only in Britain, but throughout the earth. They reflect a man-made world. In 1980 the United Nations declared: 'Women comprise 50% of the world's population, do two-thirds of the world's work hours, receive 10% of the world's income, and own less than 1% of the world's property.' What an exposure of the subjection of women! The figures are so stunning that I must repeat them. *Half the population do two-thirds of the work, get only 10% of the income and own only 1% of the property*. It seems hardly necessary to provide any more evidence that the earth is male-dominated.

Of course this is a world picture and not necessarily applicable to Britain. Probably the severest inequality occurs in Africa and Asia. I remember how shocked I was in Kenya in the 1950s to see women carrying heavy loads on their shoulders while their husbands walked behind carrying nothing. I was outraged by what was called women's circumcision, destroying sexual pleasure of the clitoris in order to discourage intercourse by unmarried virgins. Both these practices have been modified, but the subjection of women remains rife throughout Africa. The Third World needs a women's revolution.

That accepted, the facts cited in what follows prove that in Britain women are also subjected. The same is true of all the industrialized countries, but Britain is probably the worst among them. Compare the status of women here with the situation in the United States of America. The USA has women Supreme Court Judges; we have no woman judge. In America there are women presidents of banks and directorships held by women are common. Here? It is not only the elite who are thus privileged in the United States; it is generally accepted there that working women will have serious jobs for most of their lives. I am not suggesting that all is well in the USA. The fundamental basis of male domination in its political, cultural, social and economic structure remains. But in Britain it is more unrelieved.

Let us look at the broad position of working women here. Over 40% of our workforce are women. Over two-thirds of single women are in jobs or seeking jobs, and the same applies to over half of all married women. They go out to work and return home to work. It is all work. As children grow up, the number of mothers working rises sharply. Seventy per cent of women aged between thirty-five and fifty-four go out to work. Working in jobs, working at home; the United Nations declaration that women do two-thirds of working hours does not seem unreasonable, even in Britain.

We have seen that approaching half the working population are women, but they are very restricted in their spheres of work. They are concentrated in the lower-paid and lower-status jobs. Their opportunities for getting jobs are almost entirely in the service industries. Three-quarters of them work there, compared with only one-fifth in manufacturing. They are the majority among clerical workers and among teachers and nurses, but their penetration of manufacturing is restricted to dwindling industries like textiles, industries supplying domestic articles and tobacco. Large expanses of industry are monopolized by men.

When it comes to payment and status the inferior treatment of women is glaring. According to government figures, women receive on average 40% less than men, which is probably an underestimate. In 1979, half the nation's women workers were paid wages under the poverty line. The children in their homes suffered. Between 1977 and 1981 the number of children in poverty, or on the margin of it, rose to the appalling figure of three million. In 1980 male manual workers received on average £111 gross a week (itself disgracefully low) and women £68 a week. Need one write more?

As for status, how many women are directors or managers? Seventy per cent of office workers are women, 99% of typists and secretaries, but women managers number only 14%.

In the recession of the 1980s, women suffered most. It meant an end to any expansion of employment and women were the first to be sacked. Thousands of married women workers who lost their jobs did not register as unemployed. Sixty per cent had not paid full National Insurance contributions and had no right to benefits. As married women they could not get supplementary benefits. In 1982 10.7% of families with dependent children were headed by lone mothers. Their plight was even worse. Ten per cent of *all* children at that date were looked after by lone mothers, far more of whom worked than married mothers, mostly for very low wages. By 1985, half the homeless were one-parent families.

Discrimination against women takes place in nearly all spheres of life. Ms Jo Richardson MP, the Labour Party spokesperson on women's rights, pointed out in 1985 how it occurred in the social services and taxation. The Chairman of the National Council for Voluntary Organizations wrote to *The Times* exposing inequality in the Community Programme. Trade-union administration is often guilty. The immigration regulations are weighted against women.

The facts of discrimination have become so widespread that they are recognized in legislation. An Equal Pay Act was passed in 1970, a Sex Discrimination Act in 1975, and an Employment Protection Act in amended form in 1977. The Equal Pay Act proved less effective than was hoped. It required that when a woman did the same work as a man she should be paid the same wage, but most women do a different kind of work and consequently there was no basis for comparison. Thus only a small minority of women benefited, perhaps 10%.

The Sex Discrimination Act widened the area of equality from wages to several comparable relationships, such as application for jobs, promotion, housing and access to places used by both sexes, except private clubs. It was similar to the Race Relations Act, an acknowledgement that women are deprived as well as blacks. A considerable number of women benefited, but only a small fraction of the whole.

The Employment Protection Act introduced women's redundancy payments and maternity benefits but required conditions of service which excluded over one million workers. To benefit, a women had to work either sixteen hours a week with two years' continuous service or eight hours a week with five years' continuous service. It was the insistence upon continuous service which excluded so many women. And under Mrs Thatcher the conditions have become increasingly harsher.

Until 1985 Wages Councils guaranteed many workers a minimum wage, but a large number of employers ignored the requirements, which were in any case severely restricted by the Government in 1985. It was stated that, in 1984, 9,842 employers were known to have broken the law. Only two were prosecuted! Incredible. A factor is the absence of inspectors of wages and conditions. In the clothing industry in London, legal requirements are frequently broken, as they are in other low-paid industries where the majority of workers are women. However, the legislation against sexual discrimination was of value, despite its limited effects, in influencing the climate of public opinion and in endorsing a principle which could be carried further in future measures.

What should these measures be? First, the present discrimination in welfare, taxation, immigration and other spheres should be ended. Second, nursery schools should be established everywhere to enable married women and single parents to go to work when they desire to do so. Third, all companies doing work for the Government or public contractors should be required to abide by a code of equality for women, in recruitment, training, wages and promotion. The Greater London Council gave a good example in insisting that all suppliers and contractors carried its Equal Opportunities clause which applied to women, black, Asian and disabled persons. Fourth, the statutory minimum living wage which has been proposed earlier should of course apply equally to women and men, thus lifting thousands of women from poverty. Fifth, in my view something more controversial should be accepted. Present discrimination is so great that if equality is to be secured there should be for a period positive discrimination in favour of women. When equal abilities between a woman and a man are shown, the choice should go to the woman.

After all that has been written above, let the fact be emphasized that companionship between men and women is one of the best features of our society. In many families there is deep partnership between husband and wife. Many single men and women have a similar relationship, working together, conversing seriously when they meet on every kind of subject. That recognized, the truth is that most men, inheritors of centuries of tradition, still think and act (subconsciously if not consciously) as though women were subservient to them. A woman friend summed up for me the four basic needs which men want fulfilled by women: first, to satisfy them sexually; second, to provide and bring up children; third, to provide food and comfort; and fourth to give care during illness and old age. In return, men were once expected to provide financial security, especially during child-rearing years, but now women are contributing substantially to that, and are often forced to fend for themselves. In general, men take more than they give.

The fundamental necessity is to recognize that

women have personalities as well as men and that they should have an equal opportunity to fulfil them. They have as much right as men to express themselves in what they do. They fall in love, want children, and generally accept the duty of looking after them, but that does not mean that their desires and talents should be permanently suppressed. As we have seen, the majority of married women go out to work. This is not only to increase the family income, although that is often necessary; it also reflects their wish to be doing something positive, to be participating with others, to feel self-respect and equality. But, as we have also seen, women have little opportunity to fulfil their desires or potential abilities. Their work is restricted and payment low. They live in a man-made world and rarely have the chance to express the contribution which they could make to the benefit of us all. Admittedly, most of this is true of men as well. We need a new social order. But women suffer more.

I must conclude with a confession. I have been guilty. Theoretically I have stood for women's equality, but I too have inherited man's history. A friend of mine overheard, at the bar in the Guest Room of the House of Lords, a group of male peers speaking appreciatively of me. She wondered what a group of women would have said. That made me think. Perhaps they would have appreciated some of my public activities but if they had been frank what *would* they have said of my attitude to them? I have been served by devoted women all my life. I have accepted it, sometimes doubting because I gave so little in return. What have I given them? I am afraid I must say that these have been limited partnerships, not equality in practice or depth. We men are the prisoners of all time. It is not only women who need a revolution. We all do.

5

Imperialism Remains

Perhaps the most spectacular achievement of the aims which I have supported from the beginning of the century was the colonial political revolution in the twenty years following the Second World War. I was an anti-imperialist even before I joined the Labour Party. I remember applauding Campbell Bannerman, the Liberal leader, for saying at a meeting in Caxton Hall in 1906 that bad administration under self-government was better than good administration under alien government.

With Keir Hardie's leadership, ILP approaches to imperialism concentrated, before the First World War, on British occupation of Ireland, India and Egypt. An interview which I had with a representative of the South African Native National Congress after the First World War appeared in the *Labour Leader* and initiated the campaign against apartheid in Britain. In 1919 I was the last joint Secretary of the British Committee of the Indian National Congress. I moved the resolution at a Labour Party Conference in 1925 which committed the party to the independence of India. I was the first Chairman in 1928 of the League Against Imperialism, uniting Third World leaders with Europeans. I was suspended from Parliament in 1930 for protesting, out of order, against the imprisonment of Mahatma Gandhi, Jawaharlal Nehru and thousands of Indians. Then the anti-imperialist struggle turned to opposition against the racist tyranny of Hitler.

After the Second World War I was the Chairman of the Congress of Peoples Against Imperialism, an international organization with its secretariat in Paris, which had an extraordinary effect in uniting nationalists in territories occupied by the French and British with the growing movements here and in France. When the Congress office in Paris was closed during the Algerian war we established in Britain in 1954 the Movement for Colonial Freedom, which has been described as the most influential pressure organization of the century.

I am embarrassed in recording all this personal activity, but I suppose until Asian and African political independence was won I was known most as an anti-imperialist. It was my hope for fifty years.

I tell first of my association with Third World leaders. I have written that the greatest privilege of my life was my association with Mahatma Gandhi. After I had moved the resolution in 1925 which committed the Labour Party to the independence of India, Gandhi invited me to attend the meeting of the Indian National Congress in Madras at Christmas 1927. On the eve of the meeting I was badly injured in a motor accident. Gandhi came to see me each day in hospital. In 1929, Vallabhai Patel, who had been Speaker in the Indian Legislature, asked me to do research for Gandhi on the practice of non-violent Non-Co-operation. Later, I was among those who met him at Folkestone when he attended the Round Table Conference in 1932 and my little daughter Olive presented him with flowers at a great welcome gathering in Friends'

House. He kissed her on the forehead and for days she refused to wash it off. Gandhiji, while he stayed at Kingsley Hall in East London, had a rudimentary office in Kensington. One of the most memorable experiences of my life was sitting with him opposite his spinning-wheel when we talked of all the problems of life. We discussed religion. When I remarked that I thought Christian ethics were the highest, quoting Jesus as saying we should love our enemies, Gandhi said quietly 'I have no enemies.' I told him that while I believed in a spiritual universe I was an agnostic regarding a personal God. If there were a God, who created Him? Gandhi's answer has impressed me ever since. 'We are not infinite creatures,' he said. 'We are finite beings and can speak only of what we have experienced. Thousands of people of all religions have experienced communion with God. We know He is a Reality. The explanation of your question is beyond our experience. It is infinity. We cannot know.'

I differed from Gandhi on a number of issues. For example I think it was futile for him to oppose industrialization, inevitable despite its injustices. An exception to this was the Tata Company, now so powerful. This company applies Gandhian principles. It employs untouchables, encourages co-operation, and not only pays high wages with good working conditions but sets aside 81% of its profits to trusts serving the community.

I also differed from Gandhi on sex, which he seemed to regard only as a carnal exercise to satisfy physical appetites. Often it is that, but sexual intercourse can be a deep spiritual experience, woman and man floating together to eternity.

I first met Jawaharlal Nehru in 1911. He was a student of law in London but came to Oxford to hear me speak on Indian independence. I was amused to read in his biography that he thought I was extreme; he was still under the influence of his father, Motilal, the moderate leader in the Legislature. Although he was not committed to non-violence he revered Gandhi and was utterly loyal to him during the struggle for independence. Inevitably he became the first Indian Prime Minister. Our association then became close. Visiting London, he stayed in our home, so charming to the children that they didn't want to go to bed. We spent the greater part of the night discussing the world, my poor wife Lilla having to make tea every half-hour.

My first contact with Indira Gandhi was when she was a student. Jawaharlal brought her to tea. Those who knew her later won't believe this, but she was shy and speechless. I was deeply critical of her first period as Prime Minister, when she imprisoned Jaiprakash Narayan whom I revered, and many of my Socialist friends. I came to admire her as greatly during her second term. Her speeches on international issues were the noblest of any statesman and she did a remarkable job in getting the Conference of Non-aligned Nations to adopt disarmament and development as their first objectives.

As I shall tell later, in August 1984 Indira spent an hour with me and my colleague, Margaret Glover, planning action for peace. Her assassination was a shock. I first met her successor, her son Rajiv, at a family dinner to which Indira invited me and my daughter, Joan Pover in 1978. He impressed me by his quiet approach to issues.

When I turn to Africa I think first of Kwame Nkrumah. He was Prime Minister of Ghana, but he should have been the leader of all Africa. His plan for Pan-Africanism, subordinating all the new states to a federation, would have saved its peoples and all of us from many disappointments. When he was still a student he used to come to a

Soho basement run as a club by young Indian nationalists. A weekly meeting was held there of young Africans planning their struggle in their respective countries. (They nearly all subsequently became Prime Ministers or Presidents.) One evening Kwame told us that he had been invited to return to Ghana to lead its national organization but was doubtful because it was bourgeois. It was George Padmore who convinced him that he should use the opportunity to bring in the workers, peasants and youth. Padmore, after drafting with Lenin the Communist International Manifesto, resigned from the Communist Party when it modified its anti-imperialism in order to secure a Popular Front in the thirties.

Kwame was in prison when he was elected Chief Minister. An English civil servant told me that under him he had to do more work in one year than in the ten years before, and the Governor confirmed to me his reforming ability. Kwame was too kind. In an hour's walk, arm in arm, I warned him of the machinations of some of his colleagues. 'I cannot dismiss them,' he said. 'When I was homeless they gave me a bed and food.' Deserted by his colleagues and betrayed by his lieutenants he became a lonely man. He, too, was assassinated. Ghana and Africa are now beginning to realize his worth.

I co-operated with many who became leaders in Africa and the Caribbean. Of three I should write. Before going back to Nairobi, Jomo Kenyatta conducted his campaign in Britain through the ILP and I spoke at many meetings with him. He was a great favourite at our summer schools, with his spear and African dress. His first wife he met in the ILP. Although he was found guilty I am doubtful whether he initiated Mau Mau, the violent campaign against British rule. He invited me to his farm when he became President, proud of his hundred women dancers, but I was disappointed by his record. His family became corruptedly rich. Nevertheless Kenya owed its independence more to him than any man.

I knew Kenneth Kaunda, President of Zambia, when he was a young man in London. He was a gentle soul, a pacifist by nature. I called him the Gandhi of Africa. In office he was distressed when he had to repress violence by violence. My daughter Joan and I were his guests in Zambia in 1978, a kindly host. It was remarkable how he retained the confidence of his people through a series of crises which would have brought many down.

My most loved African leader is Julius Nyerere, ex-President of Tanzania. He was Socialist in his lifestyle. He refused all the luxury which his post offered, living simply, driving his small car without the cavalcade which usually clears the road for Presidents, stopping at the red lights like everyone else. I stayed a weekend at his small farm retreat near Lake Victoria and was touched by his equal comradeship with all. His country had great economic difficulties, but he constantly rejected the demands of the International Monetary Fund that he should cut his social services to the poor. I met him in London on the eve of his resignation as President and he was as vibrant and confident as ever. I pray that Tanzania will win through.

The Tunisian leader with whom I was most closely associated was Habib Bourguiba. By accident I became involved in the treaty with France which preceded Tunisia's independence. Addressing the Tunisian trade-union congress in 1951 I put forward proposals for a settlement with France and to my surprise when I returned to London, Pierre Mendès-France, the Prime Minister, telephoned asking me to send him them. Negotiations then began but the Tunisian delegation insisted on the release of Bourguiba from detention before they would accept the French terms.

Bourguiba contacted me and implored me to press the delegation to accept without his release. I spoke to the French Premier's secretary, who assured me confidentially that a signature would soon be followed by Bourguiba's liberation. I then saw the Tunisian delegation in Paris and without revealing what I knew got them to agree, in view of Bourguiba's own wish and for the sake of Tunisia, to accept the treaty. An astonishing event followed. Bourguiba came to see me in my home in London and invited my wife and me to dinner. We went thinking it would be *tête-à-tête*, but were surprised to find several members of the Tunisian Cabinet there on a very formal occasion to thank me and two others who had served Tunisia. More than that, after dinner Bourguiba gathered his colleagues in a circle and presented the Order of the Republic of Tunisia to me, pinning it on my chest. I cherish it but have never worn it.

I find I have recorded an event rather than a personal portrait. I return to events. I have described elsewhere my activity for peace in Vietnam. Hanoi was the second Government to present me with an order, which I handed over to the British-Vietnam Association, whose Chairman and Secretary, David and Joan Yuille, served so marvellously. The USA Government revised their policy after the massive resistance in their own country to the war with Vietnam. They decided not to send troops with inevitable casualties to invade territories whose regimes they disliked but instead to provide arms to the rebel forces. Others would kill and be killed, not their own citizens. This they are doing in the case of Nicaragua. How they reconciled their actions to their protest against the Soviet intervention in Afghanistan one does not know.

The one exception to the revised policy was the American invasion of Grenada, an outrage so great that even Mrs Thatcher's Government, so obedient to President Reagan, dissociated itself from it. The use of troops in this case reflected the small force they had to overcome. I was deeply distressed by the assassination of Maurice Bishop. When he was a student in London I saw him many times and he called himself my pupil. Another head of state whom I influenced in youth was Siaka Stevens of Sierra Leone. He succeeded in holding his disparate country together remarkably.

I confess I was severely disappointed by what happened over a great part of Africa after political independence was won. There had been seventeen military coups by 1985. There was a great gulf between the ruling class, whether military or civilian, and the people. The Governments and the armed forces were controlled by elites who had been educated and trained in Britain or the United States; British and American Africans, not African Africans. They lived in the style they had learned in London and Washington, so different from the poverty of the millions they ruled. There were exceptions, where Governments sought to raise the standards of the people, for example Tanzania, Zambia, Zimbabwe, Senegal and, almost certainly, the Congo, Angola, Mozambique and Ethiopia, although I have not visited these latter countries and do not know in depth. But for most of Africa poverty among the masses continued, and even grew, under the independent Governments.

Kenya was a particular disappointment to me because I had been so closely associated with its struggle for independence. Corruption and nepotism became rife under Kenyatta's rule, and little was done to end poverty. When President Moi followed, he began well by standing for human rights, but I was shocked on my visit in 1978 to find how poverty remained. Nairobi and Mombassa gave an entirely false impression of prosperity, although even there areas of deprivation existed.

Nevertheless, the political revolution was a progressive achievement. There was more violence in Europe when empires gave way to national states than there has been in Africa. Its peoples, as education spreads, will pass through this stage just as European nations have done. We, too, have not conquered inequality, and our opportunities are greater. We cannot be self-righteous.

The overall picture of Africa is even more depressing than the failure of its rulers. Political imperialism may have gone, but military and economic imperialism is more dominating even than in colonial days. The West and East are pouring arms into Africa. The annual average figures for imports of major weapons to all Africa (1980–3) was 2,506 million US dollars. Of this thirty-three million US dollars consisted of imports to South Africa.

The superpowers and their allies are rivalling each other to impose themselves on Africa, to win support from the new nations and to arm them in preparation for a global war. Thus Africa is becoming a part of the confrontation in the world. There are also reasons why African Governments themselves desire arms. The first is the desire for military strength to match South Africa. The second is because many of the Governments have succumbed to the myth that military strength is the measure of power and prestige. Thus they become partners in the military imperialism and the deluge of arms which the industrialized nations pour upon their peoples. Their purchase of arms is one of the causes of their failure to deal with poverty. They have no money left for construction, especially in agricultural development.

Economic imperialism has become stronger through the expansion of multinational companies, based mostly in America but also in Britain. In

1983 Barbara Dinham and Colin Hines published *Agribusiness in Africa* (Earth Resources Research, £4.95) which describes in great detail the activities of the multinational companies in agriculture. It begins with ownership of plantations. Many Governments have now nationalized these, but because of the lack of African technicians, officers of the multinationals continue to manage them and make greater profit than before in processing, trade and transport. Economic domination has gone much further. Multinationals have invaded everything; manufacturing, wholesale and retail trade (even supermarkets), exports and imports, banking, insurance. The authors deal with agriculture, but their facts are becoming increasingly applicable to other spheres. They show that in 1983 eight multinationals held about 90% of tea marketing in Europe and North America, that six controlled between 89% and 95% of the world leaf tobacco trade, that four controlled 60% to 80% of world cocoa sales, that one company bought about 96% of the sugar imported into the EEC, and that sixteen companies dominated 85% to 90% of the world cotton trade. These were mainly old-established companies. The newer multinationals, based mostly in the USA and Britain, are now moving in to control manufacturing and general trade in a similar way. The Soviet Union and China have extended economic interests in Ethiopia, Mozambique, Angola and Tanzania. Africa is becoming an economic colony with alien nations dominating life to an even greater degree than in colonial days.

The trading arrangements between the industrialized countries and Africa, indeed the Third World, were decided at a conference at Breton Woods in 1944. This was before the wave of independence following its achievement in India in 1947. The nations of Africa and Asia had no self-governing representatives at the conference.

The inevitable consequence was that the decisions were heavily on the side of the industrial powers. There was some benevolence under the influence of J.M. Keynes, but two years later this was being ignored. The World Bank and the International Monetary Fund dominated loans for development, and the expanding multinational companies increasingly dominated production and trade. The African Governments piled up huge debts in the purchase of arms and in other imports and had to meet the heavy cost of paying interest. Africa was becoming economically enslaved.

Meanwhile, millions of people exist in sub-human poverty; thirty million annually die from starvation and medical neglect. The industrialized nations do little in aid. They set 1.7% of their gross national product as their target and many do not even reach that. In his powerful reports Willy Brandt pointed out that a fraction of 1% of the world's military expenditure could end poverty in the poorest countries within a decade. Then in 1985 came the disastrous drought in Ethiopia which brought death to hundreds of thousands. Western Governments acted with some generosity in view of the fact that Ethiopia had a Communist administration, and the people, certainly in Britain, responded to the need with remarkable activity.

But the aid was too little and too late. Christian Aid had warned a year previously that the calamity was coming. In the Lords I repeatedly urged that the World Agricultural Organization should be instructed to watch and report when famine was looming and had some assurance that this would be done. I had no response, however, to a proposal I made over several years that the United Nations should have a permanent relief force with food and medical supplies in stock, and planes, doctors and nurses on call, to meet an emergency when it arose.

Aid is necessary, but it is not the solution. As we

have seen, the basis of world economic relations is wrong. In 1973 representatives of seventy-seven nations meeting in Algeria prepared the first draft of a New International Economic Order (NIEO). It has been progressively developed and is now supported by 130 countries.

The basic principle of the NIEO is that a co-operative partnership should be built up between the industrialized nations and the Third World. They should have equal representation on the international finance institutions so that distribution of loans could be based on what the receiving nations need instead of on imposed conditions. At present the International Monetary Fund insists on reduction of expenditure on social services if a loan is to be granted; the World Bank has been less capitalist-minded. The Committee of Seventy insisted that partnership in reaching decisions was imperative if there were to be real co-operation in planning development.

Another fundamental proposal was that currency should not depend on the value of gold, but should reflect the value of actual production. I am not an economist and cannot judge how this would be done, but it has always seemed absurd to me that world currency should be tied to the value of a particular metal. The proposals for partnership went far beyond finance. It was suggested that the boards of multinational companies should have equal representation from the administrations of the countries in which they operated. It was also suggested that a code of conduct should be adopted under which the African workers would be assured of a living wage, trained for skilled work, and promoted as they became efficient up to the rank of management, and that consultations should take place with representative trade unions about matters affecting the conditions and prospects of the workforce.

There was also the proposal that wholesale and retail trade should be governed by partnership. As multinational companies increasingly control both, equal representation on their boards would ensure this. I have not seen a proposal that consumers should be given representation. This emphatically should be considered.

Partnership is also advocated in the important field of transport, not only within nations but between the Third World and the industrialized countries. The cost of transport adds considerably to the price paid in the shops for coffee, tea, sugar, rice, fruits and other foods and also to the price paid by industry and services for raw materials. The same is true in reverse for the goods which the industrialized countries export to the Third World. The Committee of Seventy argued that the Third World should have equal representation on the management of this mutual transport.

It should be accepted that there would be great difficulties in applying these proposals. The first is the absence at present of technically trained people in the Third World to take up the responsible duties of management. And representation in control of industries and services is accepted in the capitalist West only when it reflects investment. That would have to be forgone if the Third World is to have equal representation. One finds it hard to find a solution without socializing the world economy, a distant prospect.

When this is admitted, however, the principle of partnership is sound. Discussions on its extension have gone on for eleven years in the conferences of UNCTAD (United Nations Conference on Trade and Development) and other international dialogues, but little advance has been made. The Governments of the USA and Britain have stood by the principle of capitalist free enterprise – how 'free' with the vast multinational companies? –

which is making Africa an economic colony. A new attitude is imperative. We must at least begin the creation of a New International Economic Order.

This chapter has been devoted mostly to Africa. The Third World also includes Asia, the Caribbean and Latin America. Within Latin America and the Caribbean the struggle against exploitation and poverty is mounting and explosions are likely within a few years. In Asia, China appears to be doing well. If democracy is to succeed in India, it must do something about its extensive areas of insanitary, primitive dwellings and the poverty of its millions of peasants. One is tempted to write about Pakistan, Vietnam, Cambodia, Thailand, Malaysia and North Borneo, all of which have problems affecting world issues, but space forbids. I must, however, refer to two more countries with which I have been involved.

For many years, in co-operation with Elsie Elliot, who would have been Prime Minister under self-government, I urged the application of democracy in Hong Kong. The answer was that China would not like it. Ironically, when in 1984 it was agreed to concede Hong Kong to China, Peking proposed an extension of democracy. Only then did the non-elected Executive agree to modify its dictatorial rule.

The second country was Indonesia, which waged a colonialist war to subdue East Timor and which repudiated human rights notoriously. When Mrs Thatcher visited Indonesia in 1985 I protested in the Lords that she had not pressed these issues. Simultaneously the British Foreign Secretary visited Poland and denounced the denial of human rights. Unhappily the issue of civil liberties is subordinate to the consideration of whether a Government supports West or East.

I have not written about South Africa, nor about

Namibia, the most explosive areas in Africa. The Government of South Africa is the only Government in the world which openly stands for racial discrimination. All the rest of the world is against its policy of apartheid - and yet it goes on. Pressure and fear of the voteless African population led in the eighties to some small reforms, but the basic wrong was untouched. The attitude of the white Afrikaner is so intransigent that one finds it difficult to foresee any solution except by violent revolution, which might involve most of Africa, a frightening prospect. In 1985 there was the beginning of civil war. South Africa defied the world by its occupation of Namibia (formerly Germany's South West Africa). Although The Hague International Court declared the occupation illegal and the United Nations Security Council demanded and planned independence, South Africa persisted, fearing that SWAPO, the militant independence movement, would establish a communist-orientated Government. The Movement for Colonial Freedom had an active South African Committee, but concluded that opposition to apartheid was outside its sphere of influence. In the early sixties it participated in the founding of the Anti-Apartheid Movement which has so splendidly carried on the struggle. I have spoken at its meetings and been continuously active in Parliament, particularly in the Lords, on Namibia. One is confident that racial equality will come to South Africa, for it embodies the creative force of our time, but only at the cost of vast sacrifice and suffering.

It is often asserted that the Soviet Union has established a new imperialism in Eastern Europe. There is some truth in this, but it is not the whole truth. The suppression of the governments of Hungary in 1956 and of Czechoslovakia in 1968 showed that the Soviet Union would not tolerate administrations which pursued policies not in conformity with its own conception of Marxist-Leninism. This was alien domination. I was distantly involved in Czechoslovakia's Government of 'Socialism with a Human Face'. One of its most prominent members, Jiri Hajek, had been my friend for sixty years and we had met frequently. We are still friends.

The Soviet overthrow of the Czechoslovakian Government by military invasion was certainly imperialist. The invasion of Afghanistan and the support given to the Polish Government in repressing Solidarity also reflected attitudes close to imperialism. But that said, there is little doubt that the governments in the Communist bloc, perhaps with one or two exceptions (of which I have little knowledge), reflect the opinion of their peoples. They are for the most part partners with the Soviet Union rather than in servitude to it. And the self-reliance of these Governments is likely to grow.

It must be recognized that the Soviet Union does little to provide aid to lessen poverty in the Third World. It contributes technical assistance to favourable Governments as well as arms, and supports in principle the New International Economic Order. But it turned a deaf ear to Willy Brandt's appeal for immediate aid to end poverty.

There we must leave the problem. It is to the shame of this generation that millions die unnecessarily in a world that has a capacity to provide all with their needs. We are still far from the achievement of a civilization in which every child born has the opportunity to reach fulfilment in body, mind and spirit.

6
The Nuclear Threat

Anti-militarism was inseparable from the Socialism I learned from Keir Hardie at the beginning of this century. He taught that it was unthinkable that Socialists should kill fellow workers in war. When the First World War broke out in 1914 I became a conscientious objector on Socialist grounds, and at the end of the war I initiated the No More War Movement which spread all over the world with vast simultaneous demonstrations. I was able to take a prominent part in the successful resistance to the attempt to overthrow the Russian Revolution, organizing action with Arthur Henderson, the Labour Party Secretary.

For a time war became less likely. The subjection of Germany was followed by Ramsay MacDonald's agreement to limit reparation payments and by Henderson's progress with collective security. Then came the rise of Hitler and the fear of Fascism. Even in these years the strength of peace feeling was evident, as revealed by the Cecils' Peace Ballot. There is a popular view that this deterred necessary rearmament against Hitler, but in his book *The Arms Race* Philip Noel-Baker exposed how disarmament negotiations at the League of Nations were sabotaged by militarist interests.

Even Winston Churchill said that the Second World War could have been avoided.

Nevertheless, I couldn't oppose the war against Hitler with the same commitment with which I had opposed the largely imperialist war of 1914. I campaigned for a Socialist transformation at its end.

A new factor was added to the character of war by the dropping of the atom bombs on Hiroshima and Nagasaki in 1945. Nuclear weapons meant the slaughter of whole populations and possibly, indeed, of all life. There is increasing evidence that the bombs, even from a militarist view, need not have been used to bring about Japan's surrender. Three weeks before the Hiroshima bomb Japan had offered peace to Stalin, insisting only on one condition: that the Emperor should not be deposed. President Truman was informed of this, but the decision to bomb had already been taken and the Japanese offer was ignored. Three hundred thousand people, including thousands of children, were killed unnecessarily and an immeasurable danger to the whole human race was unleashed.

The decision to make the first nuclear weapon in Britain was taken by the Inner Cabinet of the Labour Government in 1946. The extraordinary story of what occurred has been told by Sir Michael Perrin, Assistant to the Atomic Energy Chief, Lord Portal (see the *Listener*, October 7, 1982). Sir Michael was present with Lord Portal. Clement Attlee, Sir Stafford Cripps and Hugh Dalton were, according to Sir Michael, opposed to the construction of the bomb, which they felt would be a waste of materials and money. No mention of principle is reported. Ernest Bevin arrived late, having been detained in discussion with US diplomats. As Attlee related the view of himself and his colleagues, Bevin turned to him and remarked, 'Oh no, Prime Minister, that won't do at all, we must have the bomb.' He said he didn't mind for himself, but he didn't want any successor to be talked at as he had been by an American diplomat. 'We've got to have the bomb here, whatever it costs,' he declared. Sir Michael Perrin remembered Ernest Bevin exclaiming, 'We've got to have a bloody Union Jack flying on top of it.'

Thus the fatal decision was taken. The rest of the Cabinet was not informed. Parliament and people were left unaware. One wonders what Ernest Bevin would have thought now that we have American bases with nuclear weapons in Britain.

It was not until 1948, two years later, that Parliament was informed of the decision to make the atom bomb and it was done almost casually, as though of no special importance, in the course of a full statement on defence. There had been international warnings earlier of the danger of the bombs.

The first recorded opposition to rumours of a proposed British atom bomb was a speech by Bertrand Russell in the House of Lords in November 1945 (four months after Hiroshima), unreported in the press, but reproduced by Dora Russell in the third volume of her autobiography *The Tamarisk Tree*.

It is little remembered - indeed it is almost unknown - that the first national campaign in Britain against nuclear weapons was organized as early as 1954. It collapsed, but it gave birth to the CND and deserves historical recognition. It had become known that the Government had made a hydrogen bomb and Clem Attlee, although guilty of making the first British atom bomb, had moved a resolution in the Commons calling for a meeting between Sir Winston Churchill for Britain, President Eisenhower for the USA, and Commissioner Malenkov for the Soviet Union, to consider measures for disarmament and the strengthening of collective peace through the United

Nations. Considerable public attention was aroused and I suggested to Sydney Silverman, the leading back-bench activist in the Commons, that we should start a campaign. He energetically responded and we set up a committee which had some interesting members. The Rev Donald Soper was Chairman, and it was composed of Anthony Greenwood, Vice-Chairman; George Thomas, afterwards Speaker of the House of Commons; the young Anthony Wedgwood Benn; Canon John Collins of St Paul's; Sydney Silverman as Treasurer; and myself. Arthur Carr, an able young enthusiast, became Secretary.

We set out ambitiously after a meeting in the Commons attended by 300 representatives of churches, trades unions, humanitarian and peace organizations. We decided to launch a petition, aiming at fifteen million signatures, and an inaugural demonstration in the Royal Albert Hall. I have before me the announcement of the campaign. Its appeal might have been written today. 'We need not stress the immense issue at stake,' the concluding paragraph began:

> It is nothing less than the saving of civilization, perhaps of mankind. Science can now destroy us, and will do so, unless the moral sense of the people of the world, applied in determined and practical action, decides that disarmament, including the prohibition, under international inspection, of weapons of mass destruction, shall be realized. When that decision is reached, science can be turned wholly to its constructive task of making life fuller and better for all the peoples of the earth. This generation must make the choice - and make it quickly.

There was some controversy about the terms of the petition, many wanting more extreme demands, but it was decided to repeat the wording of Attlee's parliamentary motion. While signatures were being collected, activity took place on issues still alive today. The *Manchester Guardian* of 2 August 1954 contained a letter above the names of Anthony Greenwood, Tony Benn and myself on the effects on the population of hydrogen bomb tests by the United States in the Pacific. I remember that I drafted it. The people of the Marshall Islands, who had been placed under the guardianship of the USA, petitioned the United Nations Trusteeship Council for increased safety precautions. The British representative voted against a Russian motion outlawing further tests and an Indian motion banning further tests pending a ruling by the International Court of Justice on their legality. Instead he voted in favour of a motion sponsored by Belgium, France and the United Kingdom that if the US Government felt it necessary to hold further tests 'in the interests of world peace' (*sic*), it should reinforce safety measures to prevent a repetition of the radiation injuries suffered in the blast. In our letter we urged that Britain should have voted at least for the Indian motion. For thirty years this issue has persisted. It was in 1984 that a majority of Governments in the area decided to declare the South-East Pacific a Nuclear Weapon Free Zone.

The signatures to the petition did not nearly reach the unrealistic target of fifteen million. I do not have the figure to hand, but it was less than two million. The Albert Hall was only half-full for the demonstration. There was a heavy financial loss which Sydney Silverman had to bear, and he insisted on closing down the campaign. It was a courageous pioneer attempt and led Canon Collins to take steps to initiate the CND. Bertrand Russell became his partner and so the remarkable movement began. The pioneers failed, but they pointed the way.

I became a foundation member of the CND. The first Aldermaston march at Easter 1958 began at London and the stop for tea was at Slough, the town which I represented in Parliament. We prepared refreshments in a public park, only to be washed out by torrential rain. At a moment's notice the Methodist Minister gave us permission to use his church, where the drenched marchers dried out and drank warm tea. I didn't take part the whole way in the marches from Aldermaston because I was already becoming a little lame, but the Slough Labour Council provided accommodation in the schools and I met the marchers outside Slough.

The series of Aldermaston marches deeply impressed the public. The question is often asked why the campaign declined. There were three reasons. The first was the diversion from its original aims to opposition to the war in Vietnam. It was perhaps inevitable that the leading peace movement should turn its attention to the issue which was dominating the world, but by the time the Americans withdrew, the first objectives were nearly forgotten. The second reason was the split between Bertrand Russell and Canon Collins. Russell formed within the CND the 'Committee of One Hundred' to take 'direct action' at nuclear weapon sites. Canon Collins was opposed. The effect of this difference in the leadership was disastrous. I did not take part in the controversy, but declined to join the Committee of One Hundred.

The third reason was expanding detente, indicated by the treaty to ban nuclear weapon tests in the air. This added to a widespread feeling that the nuclear threat was less real. It was not until detente dwindled that the danger of a nuclear war became felt widely again, and the CND renewed its appeal.

The remarkable revival of the CND was also due to increased public knowledge of the effects of a nuclear war and the realization that the unthinkable was possible, even probable. Inspiration came when Mgr Bruce Kent became paid General-Secretary in 1980. The effect of the decision in 1981 by the CND annual conference to engage in 'considered non-violent direct actions' has yet to be seen. It was encouraged by the widespread recognition of the bravery of the women at Greenham Common where cruise missiles were sited. Personally I doubt the wisdom of the decision to take direct action. I support individuals who take such action from conscientious motives, but would have refrained from making direct action the policy of the CND organization. I fear it might deter the large middle opinion which, while objecting to nuclear weapons, does not countenance any tendency towards breaking British laws. I have in mind the precedent of the First World War when the National Council of the ILP defended forthrightly the right of conscience of those who refused military service, but did not advocate the action as party policy.

Theoretically, the breach of British law is justified within the CND by the conviction that nuclear weapons are themselves illegal under international law. This is a growing view of lawyers of standing. Genocide is banned internationally as a military objective. Are not nuclear weapons an instrument of genocide? To many supporters of CND, the breaking of British law is necessary to uphold international law. I address CND meetings all over the country. In eighty years of public activity I have not seen such crowds; a thousand people at local gatherings, five thousand at a regional demonstration at Plymouth, a quarter of a million in Hyde Park. I became particularly involved at High Wycombe. This picturesque town at the foot of the Chilterns is the military headquarters of the British and American forces in Britain, both of the RAF and of the American bases, and also the reserve headquarters for the Americans and NATO in Europe, to be used if driven out of Stuttgart and Belgium. It has the deepest bunker in Britain, for the military leaders. A Government survey named High Wycombe as the most dangerous place in England in the event of a nuclear war. No wonder.

It would be difficult to overstate the impact on public opinion of the CND. By 1985 it had 110,000 members registered at national headquarters and about 300,000 more through its affiliated groups. Bruce Kent became the best-known figure in Britain outside the royal family, Parliament and TV. The newspapers and TV reported CND activities or controversies about it nearly every day. The Government for a time conducted a campaign against it but every time the then Minister of Defence, Mr Michael Heseltine, spoke, the membership of the CND increased. It became the most influential pressure organization Britain had ever seen. Its Chairperson, Joan Ruddock, a winning personality, gained support by her convincingly reasoned speeches, a perfect public partner to Bruce Kent. The CND symbol became adopted by anti-nuclear weapons movements throughout the world and the CND also developed international co-operation, Joan Ruddock and Bruce Kent each travelling to distant places. A wonderful organization.

A big influence on public opinion has been made by the prolonged non-violent protest by women outside the American cruise-missile base at Greenham Common. Started by a few women from Wales, it has grown in numbers to hundreds who come and go as available. They slept first in vans and tents, making themselves a self-supporting community. They showed wonderful courage when bye-laws were changed and they were evicted, eventually three or four times a day, and forced to sleep in the open. They have gained widespread respect by their self-discipline and friendliness to soldiers, police and to the magistrates upon arrest. Thirty thousand people demonstrated their support in 1983. I took part in that demonstration (using a wheelchair for the first time in this country), but I had visited their camp several times earlier, once with Ian Mikardo and Jo Richardson. The Greenham women win repeated reports in the media, and although these are often hostile, they still bring in many recruits to the CND as the news of the new nuclear weapons spreads. When the history of the struggle against nuclear weapons comes to be written, recognition must be given to the great contribution made by the Greenham women.

I have told how I visited Greenham Common. On Easter Monday 1985, I joined the CND demonstration at the American cruise-missile base at Molesworth, where both men and women were making continuous protests. It was a desperately wet day but many hundreds were there from all over the country. The disciplined non-violent action at Molesworth has won wide respect, not least among the soldiers and police at the base. The Quakers have ensured that from the beginning Molesworth has been identified with the campaign for food for the hungry of the world, in place of expenditure on weapons.

By 1985 virtually every town and even many villages in Britain had a local peace-campaigning organization, and these, by their grass-roots activities, have kept the issue of nuclear weapons alive in the local media, while the large organizations continue to work on a national scale. Links between these groups, local churches and political parties, and organizations such as Oxfam and Amnesty International, have ensured that peace is seen not only as a matter of nuclear disarmament, but as a matter of economic justice and human rights.

7
World Disarmament

Following the death of Stalin in 1953 the climate of detente began to emerge. It was mostly destroyed when the USA boycotted Cuba, which the Soviet Union then began to arm, but Khrushchev withdrew and detente was renewed. It reached its climax, with President Carter at the White House and a Labour Government in Britain, at the United Nations Special Session on Disarmament in 1978, initiated by the non-aligned nations. Its Final Document warned of the danger of total human destruction by nuclear war and recommended a series of measures progressing to general and complete disarmament. The Final Document was adopted by the representatives of 149 Governments, including the USA, the Soviet Union, Britain, France, West Germany and China. An amazing achievement.

The principal recommendations were four: first, the abolition of nuclear weapons and all weapons of mass destruction; second, the phased abolition of conventional weapons; third, general and complete disarmament except weapons for internal security and as contributions to a UN Peace Keeping Force; and finally, the transference of military expenditure to development measures with the object of ending world poverty. The most dedicated peace advocate could scarcely have asked for more. A year later, belatedly, Philip Noel-Baker and I decided to establish the World Disarmament Campaign to realize these recommendations. The decision was made almost casually. We met in a corridor of the House of Lords. Philip, who had been a member of the British team at the Special Session, remarked that the Peace Movement was missing a great opportunity in not campaigning for implementing the Final Document. 'Let's start a campaign,' I said. Philip's eyes lit up and he shook my hand. Thus it began. We were both nearly ninety, old to start a campaign, but the response showed that the moment was ripe. We called a meeting of representatives of the various peace organizations. At first we had the support only of the Quakers, the Socialist activists in Labour Action for Peace, and the CND, though subsequently nearly all the peace groups co-operated. Important backing came later from Oxfam, which realized that while billions are spent on warfare, there is little left for welfare.

The support from the CND unilateralists was particularly welcome because our objective was world agreement. We aimed at negotiated disarmament to end conventional weapons as well as nuclear ones. We could not forget that fifty million people died in the last world war from the use of conventional weapons. The CND said that while they campaigned in the first instance to rid Britain of nuclear weapons they wanted above all to see nuclear weapons and all weapons of mass destruction abolished throughout the world. They welcomed the fact that many supported the latter who did not accept unilateralism. The World Disarmament Campaign succeeded in combining both with mutual respect. I was a unilateralist, Philip Noel-Baker was not. Never have two men worked more completely together. Strangely, we first met – it was at an ILP summer school in 1919 - to debate these two approaches.

After a launching meeting in the House of Commons we had a day's convention in the Central Hall at Westminster, superbly organized by Eric Messer, son of Sir Frederick Messer, who had been a dedicated pacifist MP. This was before the revival of the CND and was hailed by the press as marking a resurrection of the peace movement, following the decline of the Aldermaston marches. The hall was crowded from morning to night. Lord Gardner chaired the meeting and the speakers were widely representative, including Cardinal Hume for the Catholics, Donald Soper for the Methodists, Bruce Kent and Mary Kaldor, Richard Body (a Tory MP), Len Murray for the TUC, and Bill Yates for Oxfam. Philip Noel-Baker had the whole audience on its feet in response to his concluding appeal.

We began our campaign without an office or staff, but Quaker Peace and Service put every facility at our disposal at their headquarters at Friends' House in Euston Road. I worked there almost every day. Ron Huzzard, QPS's Secretary, and Grace Crookall-Greening, its Press Officer, could not have done more to help. Then support came in sufficiently to take offices in Central London and to appoint first Eirwen, and then her husband Brigadier Michael Harbottle to direct it. Michael Harbottle had commanded the United Nations Peace Keeping Force in Cyprus and he and Eirwen had subsequently been on the administrative staff of the High Commission for Refugees.

The sad truth is that after the remarkable success of our unusual convention and of the petition afterwards, we missed a golden opportunity to build the campaign. We had made a renewed impact on the public for the peace movement. We should have secured the co-operative association of the many peace and church councils which later worked for our petition. We should have held demonstrations in all leading centres to repeat the success of our convention. The opportunity was there. But the Harbottles, while they did an excellent job in winning the support of top people, had no experience in mass organization. The Liberals, Social Democrats and Welsh and Scottish Nationalist Parties indicated support. Some Conservative MPs did so and church leaders and academics were brought in. Eirwen answered all letters with sympathy and help. But no basic organization was established. We became a coterie of the elite rather than a campaign.

Our first activity was to organize our petition to the second UN Special Session on Disarmament to be held in New York in June 1982. The petition embodied the four major recommendations of the first session. Peace councils and church councils for peace were springing up all over the country and their members leapt at the opportunity of activity by collecting signatures. The members of the revived CND co-operated enthusiastically. We had the services of John Keyes, who had been London's Labour Party organizer, as Petition Secretary, and the Royal Arsenal Co-operative Society provided an office with all facilities. Eric Messer chaired the Petition Committee. We collected nearly two and a half million signatures, the largest number ever attached to a petition in Britain. Later I will describe our international activities. When the time came to present petitions to the Secretary-General of the United Nations, thirty-five million signatures were added to ours.

The First Session had instructed its Committee on Disarmament at Geneva to report to the renewed Session in New York on how its recommendations could be implemented. We kept in continual touch with members of the Committee through Frank Field, an expert in UN matters, who acted as our representative in Geneva. Philip Noel-Baker drafted a treaty which rather optimistically would have implemented the UN's four major recommendations in three stages, each of two years. It was sponsored by well-known international figures and submitted to the Geneva Committee. Among its forty representatives of Governments, twenty-one were from non-aligned nations and they became a group pressing for radical measures. The Geneva Committee adopted a policy which accepted our Treaty in principle but prolonged its periods of application. They proposed two stages of five years during which nuclear weapons as well as all weapons of mass destruction would be abolished, together with progressive reductions in conventional weapons. These would be followed by a stage of indefinite duration leading to general and complete disarmament. The group accepted the recommendation that military expenditure should be transferred to measures of development, particularly in the Third World.

We were unhappy that a target date had not been fixed to the third stage, but welcomed the broad adoption of our proposal. Unfortunately the decisions of the Geneva Committee had to be reached by consensus, and the USA, Britain, West Germany and other Western nations opposed the non-aligned plan, preferring to rely on the bilateral and multilateral negotiations on specific issues of disarmament. An ingenious method of reporting to the Second UN Special Session on Disarmament in New York was adopted. The non-aligned proposal, which was supported by a majority on the Committee, was stated in detail with objections indicated in brackets. There were many interruptions of the text by brackets, but the nature and source of the objections were not recorded. There is no doubt that most of them came from the USA, Britain and associated governments.

The World Disarmament Campaign was strongly represented with observers to the Second UN Special Session in New York, including Philip Noel-Baker, Eirwen and Michael Harbottle, Mercy Edgedale and Michael Daffern. Eric Messer and John Keyes were present with the petititon. Other WDC members included Joan Hymans for Camden Council, Margaret Glover (who accompanied me) and Patricia O'Rourke, both from Wycombe Peace Council.

Every day there were meetings of the representatives of the non-governmental organizations to review developments. We were increasingly discouraged. While the Assembly began well with an optimistic statement by the Secretary-General anticipating a number of progressive decisions, when the debates began it soon became clear that the non-aligned plan would not be adopted. The speeches from the Indian and Swedish representatives were encouraging, but it was disappointing that delegations even from some Third World countries claimed that they needed arms. President Reagan and Mrs Thatcher killed any idea of anything worthwhile happening and, unfortunately, the representative of the Soviet Union, although approving the non-aligned plan in principle, devoted most of his speech to propaganda. As decisions had to be made by consensus there was no hope of substantial results. At the end of the session the Secretary-General, clearly disappointed with Governments, said that the hope of disarmament now rested with peoples.

Three decisions were in fact made. The first was administrative, to increase the number of scholarships to students. The second may prove of importance. Early in the proceedings a decision was pushed through to establish an international educational organization to alert all peoples to the facts of the arms race. The organization was to be entitled the World Disarmament Campaign. We were flattered that our name should be adopted, but the objects of the two organizations, while complementary, were different. The United Nations organization was to convey information; ours was to campaign. Even the limited objective of the new institution was not welcomed by the USA and Britain. Both declined to contribute funds for its establishment. Pledges of finance came first from only fifteen countries, many small, but including India, China and Australia.

The third decision of the Special Session was to refer back to the Geneva Committee the non-aligned plan. This at least kept it alive and provided a focus for continued pressure.

The Special Session was followed by the terrible loss of Philip Noel-Baker. He died at his London home in 1982. Characteristically, he had stayed on in New York, addressing not only the Assembly but innumerable meetings and participating in continual discussions. He overdid it. I have told of our relationship. I have never felt more lonely than I did for weeks after his death.

Our World Disarmament Campaign was targeted to end with the Second UN Special Session, but overwhelmingly our supporters felt we had to carry on. But how? We had no office, no staff, no money. The response to this vacuum was dramatic and proved the confident vitality of our backers. A doctor, Kate McSorley, gave us the use of a commodious flat in Camden, volunteers manned our office under the leadership of Carla Wartenberg, and money began to come in. The Rev Dr Kenneth Greet, Secretary of the Methodist Church, became Co-Chairman with me, and Professor Frank Barnaby, ten years head of the world-recognized Stockholm International Peace Research Institute

(SIPRI) became our honorary Director. Lord Bruce of Donington became Treasurer. In order to avoid confusion with the UN World Disarmament Campaign, we changed our name to the World Disarmament Campaign (UK). The voluntary staff at the head office did a remarkable job. Perhaps the most spectacular success was the publication, in conjunction with the Nuclear Freeze Advertising Campaign, of an advertisement quoting the text of the late Viscount Mountbatten's speech repudiating nuclear weapons. The advertisement appeared in *The Times* and the *Guardian* on the day that the Queen unveiled a statue in memory of him. Another notable achievement was the staff's campaign, in association with other organizations, for a nuclear-weapons freeze. A large poster with an impressive design was exhibited in the London Underground and the distribution of leaflets reached many thousands. One must mention particularly, in addition to the Acting Secretary Carla Wartenberg, Peter Frankental, who edited publications, and Tony Farsky, our Financial Secretary, who later became Treasurer.

We had a Churches Committee which secured the co-operation of the Methodist, Baptist and United Reform churches, as well as the Quakers, who had been involved from the early days of WDC (UK). The Committee established a day of services and vigils for disarmament which by 1985 was observed by about 350 churches in Britain, and also in Europe. Its voluntary co-ordinator was the Rev Will Elliot, an Anglican, who at distant Chester showed great organizing skill. When the work involved became excessive, Nigel Stapley became Secretary, to assist Will. The fact that my Co-Chairman was the Rev Kenneth Greet helped greatly in winning support. Ron Huzzard, Quaker Peace Secretary, became a Vice-Chairman of WDC (UK) in 1984.

We also had a Labour and Trade Union Committee, under the leadership of Eric Messer, who organized many meetings and gained the support of the TUC and the International Department of the Labour Party. He represented WDC (UK) on the Labour Disarmament Liaison Committee until his move to Yeovil, when he asked Margaret Glover to replace him.

Our activities abroad were co-ordinated by our International Committee, of which Mary Hale became Secretary, and which contained representatives from national organizations. Its activities were immense, initiating much of what follows.

Our concentration on rebuilding the organization of WDC (UK) meant that there was at first some lack of definition in our policies. Immediate issues were arising, such as the decision of the Government to install cruise missiles in Britain and of NATO to install Pershing 2 in Europe. There was the new hope of the Nuclear Weapons Freeze movement which was sweeping America, and had captured the imagination of peace movements everywhere. The idea of a Freeze had been endorsed by the Soviet Union. There was impressive support for nuclear-weapon-free zones, which had gained a place on the agenda of political possibilities in the world. Should we not devote ourselves to campaigning on these issues?

The Executive Committee and Council adopted a policy statement which clarified any uncertainties. We insisted that the objectives of our original World Disarmament Campaign, to realize the recommendations of the first UN Special Session, and to gain world support for them, should remain our purpose, but that we should also support a series of transitional aims and co-operate with others in campaigns for their achievement. We held a meeting in the Central Hall, Westminster, on the Nuclear Weapons Freeze at which 1,500 people were present. We endorsed opposition to Cruise and Pershing 2, but as multilateralists we sought Eastern response. The Soviet Peace Committee assured us that the Moscow Government would propose no first use of nuclear weapons, a nuclear-weapons freeze, and the abolition of nuclear weapons in all Europe from the Atlantic to the Urals, with a plan for verification. That gave hope.

A major contribution of the WDC (UK) was to help give a positive international aim to the peace movement. Many of those who first came to meetings were motivated by fear of the effects of nuclear war, fear for the lives of their children, justified but negative. Our objectives opened minds to a constructive programme for peace, and especially to the use to which military expenditure could be diverted. It was striking how, as the campaign developed, the strongest applause at meetings came in response to appeals to transfer the huge cost of arms to measures to end world poverty. Development became the positive companion to disarmament.

8

Co-operation with Communists?

From the first Philip and I recognized the necessity to gain world support for the original 1978 UN proposals. Despite his physical disabilities, Philip had flown to conferences in the USA, Canada, Western Europe, Eastern Europe, Japan, Hong Kong and Australasia. It was by his persuasion that thirty-five million signatures to our petition were secured. I did not seriously renew overseas visits - I had made them often for the ILP - until Philip was no longer with us, except for attending the UN Special Session on Disarmament in 1982. But in January 1982 I was invited by the Northern Friends Peace Board to join a peace mission to the Soviet Union. It was a memorable visit, perhaps historic, both in its character and results.

Before we went the Quakers asked permission to criticize Soviet policy as openly as we criticized British policy. To my surprise, this request was accepted by the Soviet Peace Committee and we expressed our views on Afghanistan, Poland, the dissidents and conscientious objectors, not only in committee but at meetings. The only censorship was by the Soviet media which reported what we said in commendation but not in criticism.

A success achieved by the Quaker Peace Mission

also surprised me. I proposed to my colleagues that we should submit a programme to the Soviet Peace Committee for joint signature. After discussion they agreed to a draft. It began by endorsing the recommendations of the first UN Special Session, thus accepting the objectives of the WDC (UK) and then listed a series of measures leading to the simultaneous abolition of NATO and the Warsaw Pact.

When we met the Soviet Committee, its members had no hesitation in accepting our draft with only minor amendments and insisted on adding a final clause, calling on all nations to endorse the United Nations declaration that a nuclear war would be a crime against humanity. I do not reprint it here because we later agreed on a revised and expanded document.

The WDC (UK) subsequently had discussions with the Soviet Peace Committee on a number of occasions. We had no doubt about the sincerity of its members, but we also had no illusions about its functions. The Committee was not allowed publicly to advocate proposals contrary to the policy of the Government. Even when we met them a member of the Government was present, which, incidentally, added to the significance of the agreement we reached with them. They enjoyed one privilege - they were allowed to make proposals to the Government. I gathered that these were often accepted and they took special pride in one particular recommendation they had made. The Government agreed to pass a law making illegal any propaganda for war. I was able to use this later when a difference between us arose.

The probability is that most members of the Committee fully believed that the Government's proposals for peace justified support, but the absence of any right to express dissent brought difficulties of which I will tell later.

F.B. (*left*) and Philip Noel-Baker celebrating their 93rd and 92nd birthdays respectively, 1 November 1981. In the centre is Mrs Urmila Mathur of Slough Community Relations Centre. Margaret Glover in background

UN Special Session on Disarmament, New York 1982. *From left to right*: F.B., John Keyes, Eric Messer

F.B. with World Disarmament Campaign Petition signatures, New York 1982

Signing the original draft of the World Peace Action Programme, Prague 1983. *From left to right*: Professor Travnicek, interpreter, Yuri Zhucov, interpreter, F.B.

Illtyd Harrington (*left*) and F.B. arriving at Tokyo airport for the celebration of the Most Venerable Nichidatsu Fujii's 100th birthday, July 1984

ujii (*seated*) receiving a birthday present (a Wedgwood plate) from F.B. The 'enerable Terasawa is standing to the left of F.B.

Bombay, 1984. F.B. speaking at the welcome meeting organized by Murli Deora (*seated*)

F.B. with Neil Kinnock, Labour Party Conference 1984

Indira Gandhi by Margaret Glover

Tony Banks, Joan Hymans and F.B. at a GLC reception

F.B. and Dora Russell, Cornwall, June 1985

F.B. with youngest ILEA pupil, four-year-old Owen Griffith, demonstrating support for ILEA, June 1985

F.B. at the unveiling by Michael Foot of his statue in Red Lion Square

Indian National Congress Centenary Plenary Session, December 1985. F.B. dons a Gandhi cap while Prime Minister Rajiv Gandhi (*standing, far right*) applauds. 'Frontier Gandhi' Khan Abdul Ghaffar Khan is seated in the centre

F.B. with grandson David Brockway, twenty-four hours old

When in the Lords I referred to the agreement we had reached I was accused of having been duped. That emphatically was not the case. As I have written, the terms of the agreement were drafted by us and placed before the Soviet Committee without notice. We took the initiative, not they.

The following year we were invited by the Czechoslovakian Peace Committee, similar in basis to the Soviet Peace Committee, to a conference in Prague. From the first it emphasized democracy. Peace organizations in the West were invited to send suggestions for the agenda and, when we did so, they were accepted. The Conference was huge; four thousand delegates attended. They were by no means all Communist-orientated. Twenty per cent came from Eastern Europe, forty per cent from the West, and the same from non-aligned countries. Many from the two latter were no doubt pro-Communist, perhaps half.

The Conference was extraordinarily tolerant of different opinions. The CND sent observers and, although they got involved with German Greens in a disturbance, they were allowed to criticize the treatment of dissidents and of Warsaw Pact arms. I was selected to make the introductory speech on nuclear weapons, despite my reservations about Communism. It was clear that the organizers of the Conference had decided to give it a democratic tone, but the last session indicated that it was sponsored as much by the World Peace Council as by the Czech Committee. The introductory and concluding speeches were made by their spokesman. The Czechs were publicly the hosts. Their generosity was tremendous.

It was not, however, the Conference itself which was for us the most important aspect of the visit. I have told how the WDC (UK) aimed to get world support for the recommendations of the first UN Special Session on Disarmament. I have told how the Quaker Peace Mission reached an agreement with the Soviet Peace Committee. I decided to take advantage of the Prague Conference to carry forward decisively the project for world agreement on a common programme.

With my colleague, Margaret Glover (then an Executive and International Committee Member of the WDC [UK]), I had discussions with Yuri Zhucov, the Chairman of the Soviet Peace Committee, and Professor Travnicek, the Czechoslovakian representative on the preparatory committee, and they enthusiastically accepted the idea. Over several days we revised and expanded the agreement initiated by the Quaker Peace Mission and hoped it might become the basis of a World Peace Action Programme. We were televised as we signed the agreed document. I was thrilled.

We agreed that we would contact the major peace movements of the world and then circulate the programme to all peace organizations for endorsement and campaigning. Back in Britain the Executive Committee of the WDC (UK) endorsed the project but, feeling that the document dealt too exclusively with Europe, proposed additions giving it more world expression. We had ourselves realized this, even in Prague. They also felt that we should avoid giving the impression that we were imposing our draft and should ask for suggestions from the major peace movements. The Soviet Peace Committee accepted our revision of the document and our invitation for amendments. We sent the draft for endorsement or amendment all over the world. The outcome I tell later.

Differences arose in peace movements regarding our association with the Soviet Peace Committee. Professor Edward Thompson, the historian, for whom I have great regard, led in Britain the view that we should not co-operate because of the repression of independent peace activists in the

Soviet Union. He contributed articles to the *Guardian* and through the organization for European Nuclear Disarmament (END), influenced over peace movements.

We called, in 1983, a meeting of representatives of British peace organizations to discuss our differences. Professor Thompson put the view that if we boycotted the officially backed committees in the Communist countries they would change their policy towards dissidents. The discussion was remarkably good, both amiable and penetrating. I would say that most present declined to commit their organizations, but one got the impression that the majority supported discussion with the official peace committees of the Communist countries. Only Pax Christi, the Roman Catholic peace group, declared support for Professor Thompson.

END and the Bertrand Russell Peace Foundation (BRPF) called a conference of European peace movements at Brussels in 1982. I accepted an invitation to attend, and also attended the follow-up conference at Berlin in 1983. At Brussels there was no strong reflection of the anti-Soviet view and I even had considerable support for a proposal that a joint meeting of Eastern and Western peace advocates should be held in a border town. Indeed, the Berlin Committee, influential at the Brussels conference, followed up the idea, and when the proposal for a joint meeting proved impossible, it explored the suggestion of simultaneous meetings in West and East Berlin with an exchange of speakers. Unfortunately, I think, this idea was turned down by the Communists on the ground that it would emphasize the separation of West and East. However, many of the churches in Eastern Germany did hold simultaneous demonstrations.

The World Disarmament Campaign (UK) pursues delicate and double (although not inconsistent) policies towards the Soviet Union and its Peace

Committee. We co-operate with the Soviet Peace Committee and other Communist committees and at the same time denounce the repression of independent peace activists. Let me explain first our reason for co-operation.

It goes without saying that our supreme aim is peace. The Communist Committees undoubtedly represent the mass opinion in their countries. They do not need to go to their Governments directly for finance; with the encouragement of the Governments, it comes from every town and village, from factories and collectives. When I went to the Soviet Union in 1982 with the Quaker Northern Friends Peace Board - I had refused to go under Stalin - we travelled not only to Moscow and Leningrad, but far south to Tashkent and Samarkand. We were allowed to mix with the people in streets and marketplaces, and everywhere we asked for opinions about peace. It is true we did so through interpreters, but an experienced person can judge the sincerity of replies. I was deeply impressed by the passion for peace shown by everyone; it was expressed with deep emotion. Often I was told of the twenty million who had died in the Second World War, a memory passed down from grandparents and parents to children over two generations. At Samarkand we met three hundred women in a textile factory. They told us how they had gone to the management and asked that two days' pay should be contributed to the Soviet Peace Committee. I was told that this was typical. It is not only the representative character of the Peace Committees which encourages us to co-operate with them. It is the fact that they are the only means of effective contact for peace. I have told of our success in reaching an agreement on an extensive programme with the Soviet and Czech Committees. We realized that by such co-operation we could develop joint policies between West and

East with the aim of ultimately achieving unity with the peace movements of the world. Not only by meetings but by continuous correspondence we were able to maintain and increase co-operation. Sometimes we have differences but they are amicably resolved. Experience has proved that by this co-operation the gulf between East and West can be bridged, at one level at least.

I turn to our policy on the repression of independent peace activists. I think we were one of the first to protest, writing to President Brezhnev in 1983. At meetings with the Soviet Peace Committee in Moscow and Prague I personally criticized them strongly on this issue. When I was told that the independent activists were insignificantly small in the Soviet Union, with only seventeen members in Moscow, I insisted that if there were but three they should still have the right to express their opinions. I reminded the Committee that they had initiated the Soviet law prohibiting war propaganda. Surely, the implication was that peace propaganda should be legal? I saw statements issued by the independents and was moved by their appeal for trust between the peoples of the Soviet Union and the USA. They reminded me of the simple human appeals which we conscientious objectors made in the First World War. Yuri Zhucov, the Chairman of the Committee, pointed out that women protestors at Greenham Common were arrested in Britain. When I said that they were charged not with peace propaganda but for breach of bye-laws, he laughed and said that exactly the same was true of the arrests in the Soviet Union. Finally, he pledged that the independents would not be arrested for peace activities. That was not entirely reassuring but we hoped for the best.

The independent peace movements are stronger in Hungary and in East Germany, where the churches are persistently campaigning. One must acknowledge that the peace publications of the East German Government are most informative and persuasive, but the churches came into conflict with them about the treatment of conscientious objectors and the habit young people have of wearing armlets with the symbol of swords into ploughshares. At the same time the churches co-operated with the officially backed Peace Committee and did not advocate breaches of the law. It was reported that the independent activists in Hungary took the same view, but in 1984 came the disturbing news that their organization, unprovocatively named 'Dialogue', had been suppressed. We enquired the reason, but had no reply. When reports came in of the repression of independent peace activists in these and other countries, we wrote to the Foreign Secretaries of all the Communist Governments. We had a reply only from Czechoslovakia's. This assured us that action was not taken against people because of their peace activities.

It is worth digressing to consider the different priorities of West and East on the issue of human rights. Representatives of both the West and East signed the Helsinki Final Act in 1975 which included respect for human rights. The West charges the East with hypocrisy, but the truth is that the approaches of each differ. It is important that this should be understood. Communist ideology holds that the fundamental human right is life. The Soviet Union stands for full employment, subsidized food to meet family needs, and aims to provide homes for all. They point to the thirty-six million unemployed in the West, the extensive poverty due to high prices for essentials, and the homelessness of thousands, as basic denials of human rights. The West, on the other hand, while tolerating economic deprivations, tends to interpret human rights as freedom of thought, speech, writing and worship. When I put to Yuri Zhucov the difficulty we had in the West of urging a different attitude towards Russia because of its treatment of dissidents he replied that if one's house is on fire one does not enquire about the ideologies of those who come to subdue the flames. 'The world is smouldering,' he added. 'It will burst into flames of nuclear war unless we unite to prevent it, irrespective of different ideologies.' That is true, but much of the world does not realize the danger, and meanwhile the different ideologies prevent co-operation. The denial by the West of conditions essential for a full life is a basic scandal of capitalism against which many of us are striving. The denial of freedom of thought in the East is a repudiation of fundamental liberty. We need to implement both conceptions of human rights.

Differences arose between END and the Bertrand Russell Peace Foundation on the issue of co-operation with the Communist Committees. Ken Coates, the Chairman of the BRPF, told me confidentially at the Berlin Conference that he had come to the conclusion that co-operation was necessary for peace. In 1984 the BRPF broke with END on this issue, stating that they thought END was wrong not only in boycotting the Soviet Peace Committee but in opposing participation in the Prague Conference. This was very generous since the BRPF had not been invited to Prague because of their association with the Berlin Conference. Despite this difference both END and the BRPF remained associated with the Liaison Committee of many West European peace movements.

At a conference in Athens in 1984, called by the Greek peace movement, Professor E.P. Thompson and I came into direct conflict. In a challenging speech he insisted that we must regard the Soviet

Peace Committee as inferior to ourselves because it is too closely associated with its Government. I opposed this, saying that the test of superiority or inferiority should be the ability to contribute to peace. Rather to my surprise, the representative of the CND endorsed what Professor Thompson had said.

Later in the year the END Liaison Committee announced a conference at Perugia on the subject of nuclear-weapon-free zones in Europe. The WDC (UK) was enthusiastically in favour of this development and the Executive Committee appointed Roger Harrison and me to attend. Mary Hale, the Secretary of our International Committee, went at my own expense to look after me, which she did admirably. Before going, I wrote to Neil Kinnock, the leader of the Labour Party, asking whether he would confirm an assurance I had had from Michael Foot that a Labour Government would join a North European Nuclear-Free Zone (Finland, Sweden, Norway and Denmark), if formed. He sent me this comprehensively concise reply which I regard as historic:

13 July 1984

Dear Fenner,

Thank you for your letter concerning proposals to establish a zone free of nuclear weapons in Finland, Sweden, Norway and Denmark.

As you will know, within Europe we remain committed to NATO. Our aim is to establish a nuclear freeze, a strategic change away from NATO's heavy reliance on the nuclear response, and the eventual dissolution of both NATO and the Warsaw Pact.

At home, Labour remains committed to the removal of all nuclear weapons from British soil and waters as an integral part of placing our country's defences on a sound, non-nuclear footing.

I am therefore happy to endorse the previous comments by Michael Foot and to state our willingness to be associated with other European Nations in an attempt to create within Europe an expanding zone that is free of nuclear weapons.

Yours fraternally,
Neil

Some of us will disagree with Britain's membership of NATO but the assurance of association with European Nuclear-Free Zones was clear and emphatic.

It was good to meet at Perugia representatives of peace movements in North, Central and South-Eastern Europe, and to hear of their plans and their campaigning for Free Zones. They co-operated in proposing a corridor between them across Europe and one welcomed their assurance that they did not advocate increased conventional arms to replace the nuclear ones. But this was the only good thing about the conference. Interest in the Free Zones was subordinate to a continuous demonstration of anti-Soviet feeling.

Although Ken Coates was presiding, anti-Soviets unofficially took possession of the Conference at the first plenary session, with a banner stretched the whole length of the platform and with four groups on the platform itself, which were supposed to represent the independent peace activists in Communist countries. There was justified indignation that the independents invited to the Conference had been refused visas. A delegation of observers was present from the Soviet Peace Committee; they behaved with commendable restraint. I was not called during a discussion on East–West relations, but in an open-air demonstration at the astonishing time of eleven o'clock at night I was able to urge that, while protesting against the treatment of independents in Communist countries, our first duty as citizens of the West was to agitate against the wrongs our own Governments committed. I cited the British action at Diego Garcia in the Indian Ocean, where in 1973 we exiled the whole population to make way for an American military base.

The END Liaison Committee organized a further conference at Amsterdam in 1985; I did not go, but the WDC (UK) was represented by Mary Hale, Secretary of its International Committee. She stated in her report of the Conference that a great deal of constructive work was accomplished. While official committees from Eastern Europe, except from Romania, were not represented, and an exiled member of the Moscow Trust Group was present, there was not the excessive anti-Soviet attitude expressed at Perugia. But despite the value of the discussions Mary Hale came to the conclusion that future WDC (UK) representation at END conferences is doubtful, since we are not eligible for membership of the Liaison Committee because of our objection to the END manifesto.

Five months after my return from the Peace Conference in Prague of July 1983, I received an extraordinary letter from a back-bench Tory MP. He stated that I was named in a leaked document from the Central Committee of the Communist Party of Czechoslovakia as having received several hundred pounds from the Communists. It was even alleged that I had replied that the money would be handed over to reliable hands. I was told that I should not assume that there was no available taped record of the conversation. I replied that there was no truth in the story and that if the MP made the allegation in the Commons, as he said he would do, I hoped he would repeat it outside Parliament where he would not be privileged. I showed the letter to Neil Kinnock who took action in the Commons. In fact, it would not have been in order because personal attacks on members of the House of Lords are not permitted. Who initiated the story in Prague? The CIA?

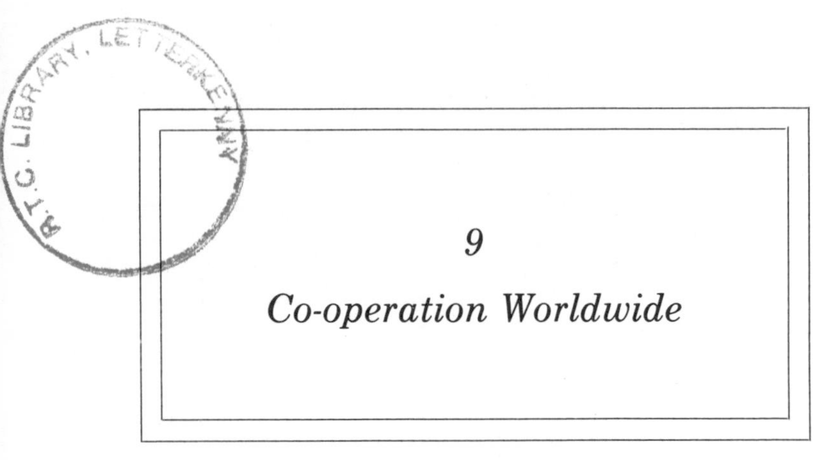

9
Co-operation Worldwide

To my relief (and yours?) I turn now from the differences within the peace movements of the world to the development of co-operation between them. Ever since the Prague agreement in 1983, the International Committee of the WDC (UK) had given its first attention to the World Peace Action Programme, which it hoped would unite all the peace movements. Discussions took place with major movements in the West and East, in Europe, Japan, Australasia and the non-aligned countries, and many re-drafts followed. Then in 1984 the Special NGO (non-governmental organizations) Committee on Disarmament at Geneva agreed to discuss it with us. Margaret Glover came with me to Geneva; she contributed valuably. She had been appointed to represent the WDC (UK) at the Athens Conference already described, which immediately followed.

The NGOs at Geneva received the proposal for developing a common programme with an enthusiasm which astonished me. Speaker after speaker in the Committee of forty praised our effort to launch the World Peace Action Programme, as an opportunity for positive campaigning. Decisions were taken to translate the programme into five languages and to send it to affiliated organizations for endorsement or amendment. A date was fixed for replies and it was agreed that the Bureau of the Special NGO Committee would meet with representatives of the WDC (UK) to finalize the document. It would then be presented to an international conference. Sean MacBride, the Chairman, even suggested they should take over the whole project but we were not willing that the WDC (UK) should be excluded.

We were excited by the decisions reached. The Geneva NGO Special Committee on Disarmament was a very representative international organization, including West and East, the churches and other faiths, and the non-aligned. At last we had found a method to secure endorsement of the final draft by a representative world gathering.

We were in for a bitter disappointment. Margaret and I attended a meeting of the Special Committee later in the year in Stockholm, and were asked to meet members of the Bureau. Sean MacBride announced that they had come to the conclusion that the decisions reached at Geneva were outside their mandate. They would provide us with the names and addresses of their affiliates and we could communicate with them, but it must be independently. Our only consolation was that when I reported to the full Committee our intention to send the draft document to all affiliates the response was enthusiastic. There was no doubt about their support.

At Stockholm we decided that that WDC (UK) should apply to affiliate formally to the Geneva NGO Special Committee. Our application was accepted on the spot. WDC (UK) has attended its meetings ever since, and new opportunities have arisen for world influence. We also aired and lobbied for the idea of a World Conference in a non-aligned country in 1986, the International Year of Peace, an idea which arose from our experience of media bias at the time of the Prague Conference.

While we were at Stockholm we made close links with the Swedish peace movement, and visited the Stockholm International Peace Research Institute. The Swedish Ambassador for Disarmament, Maj Britt Theorin, met us at the Foreign Office and was interested in the idea of a 1986 World Conference and in the World Peace Action Programme, which we hoped would provide the basis for an agenda at the Conference. We were keen that such a Conference should be held in India, and had already had initial discussions there, but we took every opportunity to sound out other suitable countries. We also had meetings with governmental delegates to the Stockholm Conference on Confidence and Security Building Measures and Disarmament in Europe. I pressed for a 'no first use' treaty, a convention on chemical weapons and a comprehensive disarmament programme.

We were now forced back to preparing the final draft of the World Peace Action Programme ourselves. We did so with the widest consultation with peace movements from all over the world, whom we invited to send amendments or express endorsement. We had a host of replies, including those from the Geneva NGOs. We considered them in detail and incorporated most of them. We then realized that some of the additions would not be acceptable to all, and decided to include a clause stating that, while all signatories accepted the broad pattern of a world in which disarmament would be achievable, they were not committed to 'work for' every item.

We were encouraged by the extended support of British organizations. At first the International Committee of the CND rejected our draft, but Ron Huzzard of the Quakers, a Vice-Chairman of WDC

(UK), got them to change their minds. The United Nations Association was at first neutral but after discussion with Lord David Ennals, their President, and Malcolm Harper, their Director, support was promised. The National Peace Council welcomed our draft with some reservations. We then had the big task of sending the finalized document to all the peace movements of the world of which we could gain knowledge. The Canadian Peace Movement generously offered help. We urged action as well as endorsement.

A new and important development in the international activity of the WDC (UK) took place in 1984. The Buddhists in Japan of the Nipponzan Myohoji Order invited me to join the celebration of the one hundredth birthday of their founder, the Most Venerable Nichidatsu Fujii. When Margaret Glover and I attended the Second UN Session on Disarmament in New York in 1982 the Buddhists had pushed my wheelchair side by side with Fujii in the four-mile march which preceded the peace demonstration of a million people. Margaret was invited to accompany me to Japan. Illtyd Harrington, the Chairman of the GLC, was also invited, in recognition of the GLC's co-operation in the construction of a peace pagoda. Of this I write later.

We were overwhelmed with delight when the Buddhists invited us to Japan. They did so with unwarranted generosity, not only in their hospitality in Japan but in paying our air fares. Joan Ruddock was also in Japan, attending a world peace conference which Illtyd and I also addressed.

The Most Venerable Fujii was a hundred in Japanese-year terms but less than ninety-eight in the Western term of years. I was beginning to rival him! We found him a charming and gentle person, given to thought and action. The celebration of his birthday was an extraordinary occasion, set in a large hall in Tokyo prepared for dinner for a thousand guests. It began with an elaborate Buddhist service, followed by a speech by Fujii and tributes from a dozen world representatives, including Illtyd and myself. We then presented gifts to him, before a luxurious meal, a film on the work of the monks and, in conclusion, massive singing by the Buddhists. I was embarrassed by the splendour.

Our visit to Tokyo enabled us to engage in much peace activity. The Buddhists arranged a number of appointments for us. We met the Foreign Minister and urged him to seek to extend Japan's no-nuclear-weapons practice to the rest of the world. I urged discreetly, Illtyd bluntly; we were a complementary pair. The reply was a very diplomatic affirmative. We met the Governor of Tokyo and suggested that the city should become a nuclear-weapon-free zone. His answer was interesting. It might become so, he said. At present the Conservatives had a marginal majority but the Progressives might change that and do what we wanted. I was highly impressed by our visit to ex-Prime Minister Fukuda, one of the most respected politicians in Japan, and also by Mr Utsnomiya, a member of the Senate, who is now devoting himself to disarmament and publishes a widely-circulated journal. I enjoyed most our visit to the one borough of Nakano in Tokyo which has declared itself a nuclear-weapon-free zone. The Council gave us tea. Illtyd and I felt that they were the Camden of Tokyo, and I suggested that they should twin with a London borough. They have written to me offering to do so and I am pursuing possibilities.

Margaret and I went to Hiroshima for the anniversary of the bombing. I was amazed by the new city which has been built. The people have left standing the ruins of a large building near the epicentre and have constructed a peace garden and museum near it. The Buddhists had arranged for me to lead in my wheelchair the vast procession in memory of the bombing, but I was overcome by the heat and had severe sunstroke. I think Margaret saved my life. She persuaded the Buddhists to get me to the main road, somehow found a taxi and while I continued to gasp desperately for breath, massaged my heart. At the hotel I was put to bed and slept for many hours. Fortunately I had recovered by the evening of the next day and was able to go to the impressive remembrance ceremony by the river. The whole population of the town seemed to be there to salute the procession of lighted lamps which flowed down the water to the accompaniment of beautiful singing. It was deeply moving. At the hotel I met the Mayor of Hiroshima and, with special delight, General Obasanjo, the Nigerian statesman who served on Olof Palme's Peace Commission. He promised to sponsor our World Peace Action Programme. Throughout our stay in Japan we lobbied for support for the Buddhist peace efforts at the London Peace Pagoda, of which I am a patron.

By a happy accident our visit to Japan was extended to India. Our outward plane journey was to be broken for the best part of a day in Bombay and I arranged to meet Murli Deora, ex-Mayor and the regional organizer of Indira Gandhi's Congress Party. He persuaded us, with the consent of the Buddhists, to stay for a week on our way back. While we were in Japan an invitation had come from Indira Gandhi to attend the thirty-eighth anniversary celebrations of India's independence, and to discuss plans for peace with her.

Murli Deora organized a welcome meeting for me in Bombay attended by nearly a thousand people. The anniversary celebration in the early morning at New Delhi was a wonderfully impressive occasion. It was in the open air and I do not know how many thousands of people were present. Indira spoke for fifty minutes from a high rostrum in a clear voice which reached all in the crowd. But it wasn't this occasion which was for us the most important. We had an hour's discussion with Indira. She proved devoted to peace, reflecting the speeches she had made on international affairs, which I have often described in the House of Lords as the noblest any politician has delivered. We discussed the idea of a world conference on disarmament, which Margaret Glover had suggested should be held as the culmination of the United Nations Year of Peace, 1986. To Indira, we ventured the proposal that the conference should take place in New Delhi.

She was responsive but asked for details of organization and finance. Margaret then proposed that we should write to the United Nations asking them to sponsor the conference. We did this as soon as we returned to Britain and also forewarned leading international figures of our hopes and asked for their support. We had an encouraging reply from the UN. They were unable to finance the conference (we had not expected that they would) but named two officials to co-operate with us if the project developed.

Indira Gandhi was extraordinarily kind to us. Amazingly, on the day of the anniversary celebrations she sat for an hour to enable Margaret, who is a portrait painter, to draw her. Indira had got up at 4 a.m., had delivered her long and powerful speech to the anniversary throng, had many other engagements that day and yet found time for this. The drawing was the last one of Indira before she was assassinated a few weeks later. Margaret gave it to Rajiv Gandhi on our return to India the following year, asking him to 'hang it where ordinary people might see it'.

The news of Indira's assassination shook me deeply. Despite my difference with her during her first period of office I had come to admire her greatly, an admiration near affection. I was not surprised by the Sikh antagonism to the Prime Minister. I had been distressed in India to find communalism growing, not only between Sikhs and Hindus, which had led to a minor civil war, but between Muslims and Hindus. It must be among Rajiv Gandhi's first tasks to re-create harmony.

We attended many engagements in India and media coverage of my visit was good. Not only in Japan, but also for much of our stay in India, we were assisted admirably by the Venerable Terasawa, of the Nipponzan Myohoji. He became, on our return, a member of our WDC (UK) International Committee.

Early in 1985, Margaret Glover, to my great distress, resigned from the WDC (UK). She had disagreed with some actions taken and as she felt principles were involved she said she must leave. I told the Executive Committee that Margaret had done more than anyone to further our international objectives. She had been with me at Prague when we first proposed the preparation of the WPAP, and at a series of international conferences developing the idea and the proposal for a 1986 world conference; she had lobbied endlessly for support for both projects wherever she went. On all these occasions, she took charge of much of the detailed discussion because of my deafness, and made many constructive proposals, as I have indicated. Needless to say, she continues to devote herself to peace locally, nationally and internationally. We remain partners for peace.

I must mention briefly some other changes in the WDC (UK) which took place in 1985. In July we appointed Andrew Dilworth of the Campaign Against the Arms Trade as our National Campaign Officer. Carla Wartenberg, who had acted as voluntary Secretary for three years, resigned for domestic reasons. We recognized that she had helped to save the campaign. In December 1984 the Rowntree Trust had given our Director, Professor Frank Barnaby, a grant enabling him to continue working for the WDC (UK) and to research into defensive arms. There had been some disagreement within the WDC (UK) over his advocacy of a defensive armaments policy by Britain, and he accepted the Executive proposal that he should now become our consultant. As such, he won confidence by his enthusiasm for the World Peace Action Programme and when in 1986 Kenneth Greet and I resigned our co-chairmanship he was elected with Tony Hart in our place.

During the summer of 1985 the Committee for Understanding in China (CAFIU), with whom we had been in friendly correspondence, invited the WDC (UK) to send a delegation to take part in a forum and to visit Peking and other places. Kenneth Greet, accompanied by his wife, represented us at the forum, and aroused interest in the WPAP. Ron Huzzard and Barbara Bowman (both Quakers), Jeffrey Segal and Mercy Edgedale (from our International Committee) were the other members of the WDC (UK) party. They were able to have useful talks with many peace activists.

In July, accompanied by Margaret Glover, I went to an extraordinary conference at Geneva, organized by the Groupe de Bellerive, an assembly of leading European figures gathered together by Prince Sadruddin Aga Khan. It was called a Colloquium and was opened by a splended key speech by the Swedish Prime Minister, the late Olof Palme. Prince Sadruddin concluded the conference, reciting the main objectives for disarmament. But in between was a series of speeches by representatives of Governments and others of international repute whose total effect was to stress the difficulties of attaining disarmament. Both the USA and the USSR were represented, the former by Vice-President Bush and an official of the US Department of Defense. There were representatives of a number of Third World governments who expressed significant opposition to the Non-Proliferation Treaty, which was due for renewal, on the grounds that the nuclear-weapon states had made no efforts towards disarmament. No speeches were permitted except by the formidable platform list, and the opportunity for questions (of which Sheila Oakes, General Secretary of the National Peace Council, made good use) was limited. Perhaps the most valuable feature of the conference was the contact we made with persons of influence, including Prince Sadruddin, Olof Palme, and Edward Kennedy. We subsequently asked them to support the WPAP.

Some reference must be made to the policy of the Labour Party, already defined in the statement from Neil Kinnock which I have reproduced. At the 1984 annual conference, the Labour Party National Executive Committee submitted a policy statement which was very definite in its commitment to end nuclear weapons and American nuclear bases in Britain. Some doubt was expressed when the party leader indicated that the negotiations with the USA might take a year, but the objective remained clear and definite. The NEC's policy statement indicated, however, that 'adequate' conventional defence would continue, and while it was stated that weapons would be defensive only, about which comment has been made, there was no promise to reduce arms expenditure, as demanded by repeated annual conferences. The way was left open actually to increase it in order to balance the disappearance of nuclear weapons. At the 1984 conference I expressed concern about this and it has become an issue of controversy within the party. One remembers that the peace movement in Europe which advocated nuclear-weapon-free zones also declared its opposition to any increase of expenditure on conventional weapons.

The WPAP was launched in late 1985, to coincide with the beginning of the UN Year of Peace. We issued a declaration to the world press and held a memorable launching meeting on 19 November in the Central Hall, Westminster. The Secretary-General of the United Nations sent a message of support and the speakers included Krzysztof Ostrowski, the Secretary of the UN Year of Peace, and Mr Garfield Williams, who voiced the endorsement of the Conference of European Churches, which is distributing the WPAP to the Christian community throughout Europe, West and East. The Rev Kenneth Greet presided and I wound up, making my speech sitting, because I had been ill for some time. The audience was disappointingly small - the night was appalling with snow and frost - but it was representative and enthusiastic. It was a historic occasion, inaugurating a common agreement to unite the peace movements of the five continents.

More than one hundred peace organizations the world over had by this time endorsed the WPAP, as well as individuals. The USA, Canada and Latin America were on the list, and so were the Soviet Union and Czechoslovakia. Western Europe was strongly represented, as were Australia and New Zealand, India, HongKong, the Philippines, Singapore and of course Japan. Africa was represented by signatures from Nigeria and South Africa. In addition eight international organizations had endorsed the programme, including the World Federalists, the Women's International League for Peace and Freedom, and the Medical Association for the Prevention of War. In compliance with the clause which states that signatories are not obliged to 'work for' every item, the Soviet Peace Committee dissented from the claim that conscientious objectors to war should be recognized, and the Czechs said it did not apply to their country. Does this mean that they have no conscientious objectors? We are now giving priority to securing the support of peace movements and countries not yet touched. We are confident of success.

On Boxing Day 1985, my daughter Joan Pover, Margaret Glover and I left for Bombay, where we had been invited to attend the celebration of the centenary of the Indian National Congress. It was a memorable occasion, with thousands of delegates crowding a stadium and representatives of sixty-five countries present. I was thrilled that the Prime Minister Rajiv Gandhi said that the Government would give priority to ending poverty in India. The failure of Governments to do so since independence had always disappointed me. I was profoundly honoured when the Prime Minister fastened on me the Indian Congress Medal, an honour which I shared with the 'Frontier Gandhi', Abdul Ghaffar Khan, who had led the independence struggle by non-violent means in a military-dominated area, and whom I had long regarded as a hero. Both of us are in our nineties. When I addressed the gathering I put on the cap which Gandhi himself had given to me, brought from England for the occasion. The Prime Minister in his speech mentioned that in 1930 I had donned a Gandhi cap in the House of Commons in a protest against the arrest of Indians for so doing.

I had hoped to take advantage of the visit to discuss with the Indian Government details for our proposed world peace conference in India, but to our dismay there was no opportunity. We felt that this would mean that the project was off, as the UN, who were also involved, needed a decision quickly. We were in despair; then a miracle happened. I remember it vividly.

While I was dictating to a journalist visitor, Margaret and Professor Thaker (who, with his wife, had assisted us on our 1984 visit and had become a close friend) went into another room to discuss the situation. They agreed that two men might help: Mr S. Ramakrishnan, Director of the Bharatiya Vidya Bhavan, and Mr C. Subramaniam, an ex-Minister and Chairman of Bhavan International. But sadly it was too late to arrange a meeting, as my daughter and I were leaving for England that night. As they opened the door to return to my room, whom did they see in the corridor, but Mr Ramakrishnan and Mr Subramaniam, come to say goodbye to me!

Although we had had no previous discussion with them on the subject, we told them of our proposed conference and the problems it had encountered. Within an hour I had endorsed their proposal that the conference should be held at Mahatma Gandhi's Ashram near Nagpur in December 1986. I undertook to initiate the raising of funds, estimated at £35,000. Margaret continued to plan the conference and discuss it with them for two days after I had returned to England.

In London I reported to WDC (UK) officers, including George Cox, who had been our representative in talks with the UN and with Murli Deora of the Indian Congress Party. Although the officers felt that the proposed conference at the Ashram was different from our original idea, and that work on WPAP must take priority, it was agreed that George should put the plan to the UN International Year of Peace Secretary, Mr Ostrowski, in January 1986. But as the Indian Government was not to be involved, major co-operation by the UN was withdrawn. It was a sad rebuff to our Indian friends who had sought to rescue our project so imaginatively.

In March came astonishing news; pressure on the Indian Government had been so great that they had agreed to sponsor the conference after all, and meet all costs. The pressure came not only from influential persons in India but also from abroad, including the indefatigable Venerable Terasawa, Fujii's devoted disciple. The government had the happy thought of associating the conference with Jawarharlal Nehru, who, as India's first Prime Minister after Independence, did so much for peace and freedom. It is now proposed that the conference should meet in New Delhi on the weekend of Nehru's birthday, 14 November 1987.

A world conference in a non-aligned country, together with the fulfilment of the WPAP, has been my dream for three years. I cannot express my delight that the conference will almost certainly take place in India.

Looking back over the years since the WDC (UK) was established I see that there is some reason for optimism. In 1984 the international climate improved. I first became conscious of this when meeting delegates to the Stockholm Conference. Antagonism had changed to personal friendliness and even perhaps to the beginning of trust. When Mikhail Gorbachev became the Soviet leader, his insistence on ending the nuclear-arms race made a good impression and hope rose that the new negotiations between the USA and the Soviet Union would have some encouraging results. Optimism must, however, be muted. The divisions between West and East are too great to expect a change without a revolution in world opinion.

The great hope is that such a revolution is occurring, already strong, becoming stronger. The longing for peace is so general in the world that, if prejudices were removed and the peoples alerted to action, the arms race could be ended. The peace movements which are the conscious reflection of this longing are themselves sufficiently strong, if they were united in their pressure, decisively to influence Governments. The summit talks in 1985 between the heads of the two supreme superpowers already represent a victory for such pressure. President Reagan and Mr Gorbachev mirrored the consensus of world opinion that something effective must be done to prevent a nuclear holocaust. One does not urge that peace movements should identify themselves with particular parties, but they must recognize that their aims are realizable only by action by Governments. There is ground for expecting that the Governments of Britain, the USA and West Germany will be changed within the next few years when general elections take place and that would transform the whole pattern of the world in relation to peace.

There are also signs in Communist countries - Hungary and East Germany for example - that liberalization will emerge and grow. If these parallel developments take place there is a basis for optimism in the longer term. Its realization will depend on the united activity of the peace movements in the five continents. The peace movements can succeed, but they will fail if they do not find a basis of united action. This is why the WPAP is so important. For the first time a common programme has been found linking West and East and non-aligned. This must be only a beginning. The present disunity is tragic. It is shown in the relationship between the World Peace Council, the International Peace Bureau, the European Liaison Committee and others. Instead of emphasizing differences between us we should be seeking the many attitudes and actions of accord and co-operate in fulfilling them.

With unity the peace movements could change the whole political climate of the world within a few years. We know of the strength of the peace forces in Britain. Three-fifths of the population are represented in 1986 by elected and regional authorities which proudly declare themselves nuclear-weapon-free zones. The CND is the largest pressure organization this country has known. In many countries in Europe - almost all, except France - the peace movements are stronger than here. In the USA the Democratic Party, strong in Congress even under a Republican Administration and likely to be far stronger after the next election, has declared itself in favour of a nuclear-weapon freeze. No one who has visited the Communist countries of Eastern Europe can doubt that the opinion of the mass of people is passionate for peace; the Peace Committees, despite their restrictions, are expressing this. The non-aligned nations in conference have declared that disarmament and development are their first priorities. In Japan thirty-five million people have signed a peace petition. Australia is taking a leadership for peace and New Zealand is giving an example to the world in action.

Nothing can stop the achievement of disarmament by this powerful movement if its different sections can find a common ground for united action. To contribute towards this is our greatest aim - to build a bridge spanning West and East, North and South. We have started on the road to success.

10

Happenings

This is not an autobiography, but I must record a few events which have taken place since I wrote *Towards Tomorrow*.

In 1983 the University of Lancaster bestowed on me an honorary degree as Doctor of Law. I told them I deserved a degree of Doctor of Illegality! Two others were given honorary degrees, Professor Boulding and Henry Moore. Unfortunately the latter was ill and could not come; I should have felt privileged to meet him.

I was selected to speak at the meeting of University staff and students on the evening which preceded the presentation. The Chancellor of the University was Princess Alexandra and I used the occasion to tell her of how the Queen helped me, when I was MP for Eton and Slough, to get a serviceman stationed at Suez to a World Championship for accordion players in Holland. She was very amused and promised to remind the Queen. The ceremony the next morning was very impressive. First a long row of students was presented with degree certificates; then the University Orator described the history of the three of us. I stood embarrassed before the cheering students and turned with a bow to receive the diploma from the Princess.

A stranger honour was bestowed on me. On the suggestion of Joan Mellors, Ian Walters, the sculptor, made a bust and full-length statue of me. The bust was shown in the Royal Academy. Tony Gilbert, General Secretary of Liberation, the successor to the Movement for Colonial Freedom, became dedicated to the idea that the full-length version should be shown publicly. When I heard of the proposal I was shocked. It would be costly and I would much rather that the money should be devoted to the movement for racial equality and peace. But the idea went ahead. The GLC endorsed it, and to my surprise the Government Department responsible for authorizing statues in London agreed. Events had gone beyond my control. Red Lion Square was chosen as the site. Ironically, I had been chairman of a committee responsible for erecting a statue of Bertrand Russell there.

The unveiling of the statue in 1985 was an extraordinary occasion. All the friends of my life seemed to be there, from before the First World War, the inter-war years against Fascism, and the post-war campaign against colonialism, as well as later companions. The large crowd circled the statue. Tony Banks, Chairman of the GLC, conducted the proceedings; Stan Newens, Chairman of Liberation, recited my doings; Ken Livingstone spoke of my support for the GLC; and Michael Foot, after praising my book *Britain's First Socialists*, unveiled the statue. I was nervous when everyone seemed to hang on my words as I replied. I said I thought I was dead because statues of people still alive are not normally erected in London. I praised Ian Walters' work on the statue, but why me? Why not Philip Noel-Baker or Nye Bevan? I expressed gratitude to Tony Gilbert and concluded with the suggestion that Red Lion Square should become a gathering-place for statues of all who served human rights, peace and Socialism. If this idea is taken up the occasion perhaps will have been worthwhile.

Another notable occasion was the inauguration ceremony of the Buddhist Peace Pagoda in Battersea Park, London. This was the inspiration of the Most Venerable Nichidatsu Fujii, whose one hundredth birthday we had attended in Japan. Believing that Buddhism is inseparable from peace, Fujii had planned to build pagodas dedicated to peace in all the capitals of the world, so helping to unite all faiths. The Greater London Council gave him a site. It was in an impressive position, in Battersea Park overlooking the Thames. Over several months a devoted group of Buddhists built the pagoda, living in bare conditions near the site. Unhappily, the Most Venerable Fujii died early in 1985 and so never saw the London Pagoda, the realization of which was his passion. His speech at his birthday celebration had been almost entirely devoted to it. It was the seventieth pagoda the Order had built. The Venerable Terasawa, his devoted colleague, succeeded in getting representatives of nations all over the world to attend the opening. The Pagoda is a beautiful construction and every part of it reflects dedication. To me, more remarkable than the international representation at the opening ceremony was the identification of all faiths. My ancestors were Christian missionaries in Asia and Africa, believing that all who were not Christian were heathen. Yet here Bishop Huddleston presided, and Anglican and Catholic spokesmen and representatives of the other faiths, even American Indians, joined in, recognizing that Truth is not confined to Christianity or any other faith. This reflected a revolution in religious thinking. I was glad as a Humanist to add my tribute.

In the same year I was invited to unveil a plaque, on the house in Highgate where he had lived, in memory of Veer Savarkar, a pioneer of the demand for Indian independence. He campaigned with Tilak before the Indian National Congress endorsed independence. The unveiling was an impressive occasion, attended by the deputy-leader of the GLC and other local representatives. I was particularly pleased to meet Sunil Gavaskar, the Indian cricketer, introduced as the best batsman in the world. He was very attractive and charming.

I also unveiled a plaque to Sol Plaatje, the founder of the African movement for equality in South Africa, and the father of the anti-apartheid movement in this country. Representing the Native African National Congress, which he established ('Native' was afterwards dropped), Plaatje came to London in 1914 to make public opinion aware that the Afrikaner government was adopting the fundamentals of apartheid. The British, involved in the First World War, showed no interest. It was not until 1919 that an interview which he gave me for the *Labour Leader* alerted activists to what was happening. Questions were put in Parliament; agitation began.

The plaque in Plaatje's memory was placed on the terraced house in Walthamstow where he had stayed. Paul Boateng, the GLC Race Relations Officer who initiated the placing of the plaque, was glad that it had been erected before the GLC was abolished.

I was outraged by the Government's decision to abolish the GLC and other metropolitan councils. Many of them were giving a lead for Socialism. The GLC stood for all the basic values - against unemployment, racialism, women's inequality and for disarmament and peace. County Hall became a palace of the people. I felt so keenly that I stayed at the Lords late at nights to vote against the Government. The admirable Inner London Educational Authority was also threatened. They arranged for me to meet their youngest pupil, a boy of four, to reflect that childhood and age were united. I had a charming letter from him afterwards. We were much photographed.

A change took place domestically. As I grew older I needed increasing attention and it became too much for my wife. In 1982 we reached a friendly agreement that I should accept an invitation from my daughter, Joan Pover, to join her in her flat at Bushey. My relations with my wife remain amicable and she comes to see us and phones often. I can never forget the long years of co-operation we had and her devoted care of our son, Christopher.

Joan looks after me wonderfully. She is active in the Woodcraft Folk Movement, which encourages children of both sexes to live together co-operatively and grow up with a sense of fellowship with all races, and to devote themselves to peace. Our living-room has a patio which looks out on a garden with four fir trees bordering flowers and grass, which has become my church. The garden has developed into an aviary, the birds encouraged by the food which Joan offers them. There are twenty-nine varieties, from the proletarian sparrows to the streamlined collared doves. We know many of the birds individually. I could write a book about them; watching them has almost replaced television. I tell the story of one only.

We had a lonely brambling. Usually they come in flocks and fly to a cold country in the summer. Ours stayed for three summers, hiding in the shade of a tree during the day and coming out in the evenings. We think it mated with a cock sparrow who was its constant companion. We called their single offspring a 'spamling'. The brambling disappeared one winter – the victim of our enemies, the cats?

My living with Joan has led happily to more intimate association with my eight grandchildren and four great-grandchildren. I also regularly visit my other daughter, Olive Outrin. Joan accompanied me to the United States in 1983, where I lectured on Gandhi at Boston University. I was fortunate in 1985 in being with my son Christopher in Switzerland when my grandson David Brockway was born.

The difficulty of distance from the House of Lords is usually met by the devoted service of Joan Hymans, who has driven me to my engagements for twenty-seven years. Undoubtedly this has extended my life. As I became increasingly disabled I found the strain of travelling by bus or train too much. When Joan Hymans is not available my daughter Joan drives me, or Mary Hale. Occasionally others help.

A disadvantage of growing old is the continuous news of deaths of friends and associates. I have already mentioned some. More have occurred. My two sisters, Nora and Phyllis, died in 1980. Nora was a distinguished pioneer of women's education in India. She ran a college in Madras for training women teachers. I was glad an obituary in *The Times* acknowledged her contribution. At home, Phyllis was a teacher and a life-long member of the Labour Party. Both were very dear to me. I visited them often in their flat at Stratford-upon-Avon where they retired.

Wendy Campbell-Purdie died in Greece in 1985. She had gone there hoping to pursue her pioneering contribution to the containment of desert land. I had written a book with her, *Woman Against the Desert*, after visiting her successful achievement in Algeria of growing a forest in the no man's land between fertility and desert to prevent the latter's expansion; the Sahara advances by a mile a year.

Dorothy Dexter, my companion in peace efforts in America and Europe in the inter-war years, died in retirement in California in 1980. She had been the very able International Secretary of the Women's International League for Peace and Freedom in its earlier days. Perhaps her most spectacular achievement was to get Congress to appoint a commission to investigate the arms trade, whose report showed that armament firms fomented antagonisms between nations and then sold armaments to both. I tell the story in *Death Pays a Dividend.* We remained friends and she wrote me wonderful letters up to a few days of her passing.

The fifth death which I must record here was that of my closest comrade over many years, Leslie Hale (Lord Hale). Our association began in 1950 in the House of Commons. It was not in Parliament, however, that we established our deep comradeship. It was in Africa. He went with me to Kenya at the height of the Mau Mau trouble. We were greeted at the airport with shouts of 'Go home' and the European community was bitterly antagonistic. Leslie completely changed this psychological climate. He saw everyone of influence and won their respect. He very nearly pulled off an agreement between the legislative leaders of the three ethnic groups, European, African and Asian. He drafted an agreement and at the conference with them conducted the negotiations. Michael Blundell, the European leader, who had denounced me as a Communist on arrival, was present and under his direction the text, after detailed discussions, was unanimously accepted, with amendments which did not affect its principles. A wonderful conclusion. It was decided that the agreement should be issued to the press next morning. Then a tragic thing happened. That night the Mau Mau attacked Michael Blundell's farm. Over the telephone we heard that the agreement was off. Thus a historic event was shattered.

Leslie was not only a great negotiator, winning

sympathy by his personality; he was courageous when human relations were involved. When we arrived at Nairobi I asked him where we should spend the night - with the family of my revered colleague, the ex-President of the Kikuyu, scandalously under arrest - thus arousing European prejudice, or in Nairobi with accepted Indians? 'Of course we stay with your African friends,' he said. Leslie also came with me to Tunisia and again played a constructive part in securing independence. Immense as were his political contributions, it is as a friend that I miss Leslie most.

I cannot say how distressed I was when news came of the assassination of Olof Palme. Not only had he done so much for peace, but in his own character he expressed peace. I wrote to his widow trying to say this. Assassination is becoming a world threat. Olof Palme's death followed closely on Indira Gandhi's, which stunned me no less.

In 1980 a new warmth came into my life. I have told how Margaret Glover co-operated with me in international activities for disarmament. A Labour Party activist, CND member, portrait painter and lecturer, she came down from Lancaster to paint Philip Noel-Baker and me in order to raise funds for the peace movement. While she was painting me we found our thoughts on life and its problems were one. I visited her in Lancaster and when she moved south, I went often to her home in Marlow. I came to regard her, her mother Frances McKechnie (the widow of a Glasgow ILP-er), and her youngest son Rick, as a new family. As a single parent, Margaret has to earn her living, usually supply-teaching to fit in with her peace work and painting.

Margaret went to Cornwall in June 1985 to paint

Dora Russell, and I accompanied her. Dora was recovering from an attack by an unidentified night-time intruder who bruised her face and body severely and broke an ankle. A shocking and disturbing event which the police were investigating. Despite this she was amazingly lively, never ceasing to tell us of her experiences, ideas and hopes. Whilst Margaret painted I worked on this book, but we found time to drive around Cornwall, and were fascinated by its flowering hedges and glorious bays. I was thrilled to visit Mousehole. How often I have told how, on the declaration of the First World War, its parish council solemnly declared that it was neutral!

Alas, news came in May 1986 that Dora Russell had died. I paid an inadequate tribute to her at a memorial meeting in London.

I remain a vegetarian, a pretty good advertisement for it after nearly eighty years. Once when I went to hospital for a check-up I was asked whether I was allergic to anything. I replied, 'Yes, to nuclear weapons and butchers' shops.' I confess that I am addicted to whisky, three doubles a day. That arose from the fact that I contracted a blood-clot and the specialist said that whisky might clear it. It has. My second obvious vice is smoking a pipe, a constant companion. I have also done that for nearly eighty years.

Although I have recently devoted nearly all my activity to disarmament, I am concerned as ever about human rights, racial equality and peoples' freedom. I remain President of Liberation. In nearly every country where there are denials of liberty, imprisonment for opinions, torture and even executions, there are also committees exposing these wrongs. I don't know how many of them have asked me to be their president, though I have told them I cannot be active. I am concerned, of course, about apartheid in South Africa and the illegal denial of self-determination to the people of Namibia, and very prominent in my mind are the betrayal of Cyprus and the Israeli refusal to recognize the right of the Palestinian people to a self-governing state.

My increasing deafness has limited my activities considerably. I gave up presiding at the Executive of the WDC (UK) which was fortunate in having the Rev Dr Kenneth Greet as Co-Chairman. He is wonderfully gifted in getting through business. My inability to hear means that I have ceased to participate as a general rule in the exchanges in the House of Lords. I no longer put oral questions, though I occasionally intervene with a broad-based question. On a few occasions I have spoken during disarmament debates, once even initiating a debate, though I have to read the official report next day to know what was said by succeeding speakers and by the Minister in reply. Hardly fair! I satisfy my interest in world affairs by tabling questions for written answers. They often bring important information. I regret my deafness most because it means I cannot take part in congenial discussions with colleagues. I mostly sit alone with a drink.

The Lords have an absurd rule that no one who is not wearing a tie may sit in the visitors' enclosure on the floor of the House. The only exceptions are visitors from overseas in native dress. I tried to get this changed but a crowded Procedural Committee dominated by Tories refused even the compromise that a jacket should be worn, but not a tie. My son Chris, who dresses neatly, was removed from sitting under the Throne, a privilege allowed to eldest sons, when he was wearing a jacket and a polo-necked sweater. I said in the Chamber that this decision showed how out of touch their Lordships were with the world outside.

It is not easy in life to apply one's principles

consistently. I have found this to be the case with pacifism. I am instinctively a pacifist. It is literally true that I have never held a weapon in my hand (except a rubber bullet sent me from Northern Ireland). I think I can honestly say that I would rather be killed than kill an assailant, but the doubt arises if the assault were made on a friend. Can principles be watertight? Despite my instinct, I resigned from the Peace Pledge Union because I felt that support for physical action could not always be withheld. Although no revolt had then begun, I told its annual meeting that I would support an insurgence by the Africans to win their right to self-government in Rhodesia. I could not help supporting the opposition to Franco in Spain and I could not oppose the war against Hitler as I had the First World War. I would support a revolution in Southern Africa. Nevertheless, despite these reservations, I have remained very close to the pacifists and find myself continually supporting their demands.

Mahatma Gandhi showed in India a different way of overcoming an alien regime. There is no doubt that non-violent Non-Co-operation is the ideal method. The Africans in Rhodesia could have won self-government if they had had the mind and discipline to use it. The Africans in South Africa could do so. Hitler would never have been able to occupy Europe if the peoples had refused in an organized way to co-operate with his projected regimes. The pacifists have the solution, but the facts must be faced that the peoples are not ready to adopt it, and that the attainment of self-government and the defeat of a tyrant in war are historically progressive. That is a conclusion we cannot escape.

In a different little way I have become a Gandhian. I have got rid of any ownership of property. I have given up my share of our house to my wife, given my library to the Indian Cultural Centre, and donated my papers to Churchill College at Cambridge. I have no investments. It has meant no sacrifice; I live in my daughter's flat, sharing expenses, and I have an extraordinary sense of freedom in owning nothing. I give all I receive above the average wage in Britain to the peace movement. But in this I admit failure. As a world citizen I should defray to good causes everything above the average world income. With the poverty in Latin America, Africa and Asia, that average would be little above the hunger line. I acknowledge that I am not brave enough to face that.

For the first time since the Fascist threat before the Second World War I have wondered whether Britain will evolve through community consensus and democratic parliamentary action. Mrs Thatcher's government has created a confrontation between the people and the Establishment greater than I have ever known. It came to a climax during the 1984/5 miners' strike when all the institutions of the state were brought into action against the strikers, not only the Government but the police and the judiciary. There was a psychology of antagonism much deeper than during the General Strike of 1926, when strikers and police played football together. Added to this institutional antagonism is the violence in society. The violence at football matches is symptomatic of a much wider psychology. Not surprisingly, it is found especially among the young, expressed in the inevitably anti-social attitude of school-leavers who find after years of education that the community has no place for them. It is also expressed in racialism, which despite legislation has grown. Perhaps a deeper cause is the absence of an accepted ethic. Christian teaching has lost its influence, its good ethic along with its bad theology. And no accepted ethic has supplemented it.

Children no longer grow up in the climate of a moral code. We need a national revival, a new social conscience, as well as a Government which in its policies reflects the welfare of the whole community, beginning with justice for the deprived.

I must add something which is contradictory to what I have written. I have been humbled by the kindness of people. Perhaps this is due to the help given to me in my disablement. Almost everyone I know, not merely isolated individuals, has offered help. Kindness seems to be inherent in human nature. The isolated are those who do not have it. Our problem is to develop a society which appeals to this human quality rather than violence. I believe it can be done.

11

Inspiration

I have always loved Nature. As a boy of six years old, when I was under the care of my grandparents (my grandfather was the Manager of Lord Burton's estate at Rangemore, Staffordshire), I used to wander alone among the woods around our cottage. I can still see the beauty of the woods and bubbling stream at Killiecrankie, which I visited as a boy of ten when my parents were on furlough in Scotland. At school, with my chum Harold Hills, I escaped every available moment to explore the countryside round Blackheath (now all built up), and we were often silent in the quietude of fields and woods and streams. I will be honest and confess it was not all love of Nature. We robbed orchards and strawberry beds. But the beauty of the countryside was our basic motive for those walks together.

It was not until I had left school that this identity with Nature became a religion to me. Strangely it was at that cathedral of materialism, Blackpool, that this spiritual experience came. One evening I stood on the deserted sand, looking over the green ocean towards the red sunset. As I did so, a great calm came over me. I became lost in the beauty of the scene. I seemed to become a part of it. Gradually my spirit reached out and became one with what seemed the spirit of the sea and sky, an embracing influence. Then what I felt became even wider. I was at one with the universe beyond. Its spirit surrounded me and suffused me. Even more, I seemed to become one with all life, from the beginning of time, in the present, stretching out to the future. I was lost in it, my whole being a part of it. The sun set and the intensity of the feeling passed, but as I turned I still felt the informal presence of the experience, a deep, deep calmness: an expansion.

This experience had a profound effect on me. It changed all life. It was not isolated. It came to me often when I was alone with Nature. It swept over me as I looked out to the stars at night. I sought it in meditation. It was a continuous inspiration. I have said it became my religion. It did. I felt now that I was more than an individual. The life of all time was within and about me. I must serve it. Yes, I felt bigger, but also I felt smaller, a little person, so inadequate.

I have described my experience as a teenager. It continued throughout my life, not so often, not so completely, but with me continually, making me feel I was one with all life. Even in my old age, as I look in meditation from my easy chair at the beauty of trees and sky in the garden, I have this feeling. Only once have I felt it with another person, but it sweeps over me when I am with masses of people at a demonstration for peace and justice. Before I make speeches I make it a practice to seek it within me.

I have said that this experience is my religion, yet it leaves me an agnostic. I suppose one might describe it as communion with God, yet I have no sense of a personal God. Similarly I don't know whether there is life after death. I like Bertrand Russell's description - we are born in a spring, traverse a river, and join the endless ocean. That ocean is to me the universal spirit I have known.

My philosophy is founded on this experience. I cannot be other than a world citizen, identifying with all peoples. Compassion is not enough: that is concern by the better off for the worse off. There should not be that sense of gulf. There should be identity. I admit it is beyond human consciousness. How can one become *identified* with the suffering of the thousands who die from famine, the many who are tortured in prison? Health and happiness would depart. But it is as identity spreads and deepens that the wrongs of the world will be ended.

My sense of unity with the universe was not the end of my religion. I have described how words of Bernard Shaw had on me the effect of a conversion. When I asked him what we teenagers should do with our lives he answered: 'Find out what the Life Force - the Creative Force - is making for in your time, and make for it too. Then you become bigger than yourselves. You become a part of the Creative Evolution.' I have tried to make that my purpose ever since. I became aware of a new force in my life, a sweeping creative force. Yet I am conscious of a contradiction. I have this sense of unity with all life as it is, but Shaw's advice is to change life. Perhaps the harmony is that identity with the present is the motive for changing it for the better. Both are an inspiration. One in meditation. The other in action.

Appendix

WORLD PEACE ACTION PROGRAMME

We, the Peace Movements of the World, have different views, structures and priorities, but we are united in supporting the following comprehensive programme for world disarmament and peace. We will campaign internationally to press all governments to take urgent and effective action to:-

- RELIEVE HUMANKIND FROM THE SCOURGE OF WAR,
- REDUCE THE HEAVY BURDEN OF ARMS PRODUCTION AND PREPARATIONS FOR WAR and above all,
- REMOVE THE GROWING THREAT OF NUCLEAR ANNIHILATION.

We urge the implementation of the resolutions of the Special Session on Disarmament of the United Nations General Assembly held in 1978, which called for:

1. THE ABOLITION OF NUCLEAR WEAPONS and other WEAPONS OF MASS DESTRUCTION,
2. THE PROGRESSIVE REDUCTION OF CONVENTIONAL WEAPONS, leading to –
3. COMPLETE AND GENERAL DISARMAMENT (with the exception of weapons directed to internal security and the Peace Keeping Forces of the United Nations), and
4. THE TRANSFERENCE OF RESOURCES from armaments to world development, with the aim of abolishing world poverty, hunger and disease.

The fulfilment of these objectives will require detailed bilateral and multilateral negotiations between the governments concerned, but unilateral initiatives by any of these governments would encourage the disarmament process.

Our fundamental aim remains to arouse pressure throughout the world for the United Nations to adopt a comprehensive programme for disarmament, as first submitted by the neutral and non-aligned group of nations in the Committee on Disarmament in Geneva in 1981, and for this programme to be implemented by all the governments of the world.

In order to achieve this, we advocate the following partial measures, many of them proposals already endorsed by the General Assembly of the United Nations, but not all of us are necessarily committed to working for every one of them.

1. FOR THE PREVENTION OF NUCLEAR WAR

1.1 A joint declaration by the nuclear powers of an immediate, verifiable freeze of all nuclear weapons and their delivery systems (ballistic and cruise missiles and long range bombers) covering development, testing, production and deployment.

Freezing should be accompanied by concrete measures for reducing and destroying nuclear weapons, with the USA and the USSR taking the lead in cutting their nuclear weapons by a wide margin.

1.2 A permanent comprehensive nuclear weapons test ban on the lines already discussed by the USA and the USSR and called for by the United Nations.

1.3 A permanent agreement on the demilitarisation of outer space.

1.4 The establishment of nuclear free zones.

1.5 An agreement between the USA and the USSR and all other governments concerned on the reduction and destruction of strategic and other nuclear weapons.

1.6 The conclusion of agreements between the USA and the USSR and all other governments involved regarding the reduction and destruction of all existing nuclear weapons in Europe and the prohibition of the deployment of new nuclear weapons in Europe.

1.7 A declaration by all nuclear weapons powers that they will not be the first to use nuclear weapons, nor to use them or threaten their use against any country not having nuclear weapons on its territory.

1.8 The adoption by all states of a declaration proclaiming any use of nuclear weapons to be a crime against humanity.

1.9 An urgent international study of the possible "nuclear winter" effect, with steps to ensure that all governments and peoples are made fully conversant with its findings.

2. FOR THE IMPROVEMENT OF EAST-WEST RELATIONS

2.1 The active pursuit of detente, particularly by strict adherence to the provisions of the Helsinki Final Act.

2.2 The conclusion of non-agression pacts between all NATO and WARSAW TREATY member states in which they reiterate their promises not to initiate the use of force, conventional or nuclear.

2.3 The conclusion of an agreement on the mutual reduction of all armed forces and all armaments (nuclear and conventional) throughout Europe, starting in Central Europe.

2.4 The acceptance by the USA and the USSR of the good offices of non-aligned states in facilitating arms reduction negotiations, such as the approach of the "Four Continents Peace Initiative".

2.5 The extension of the mutual monitoring of military manoeuvres and military activities throughout the world, in order to create an atmosphere of confidence.

2.6 The eventual dissolution of the NATO and WTO military alliances and their replacement by an all European security system, sponsored by the United Nations, to which all European states – East, West, and neutral – can belong.

2.7 Agreements to curtail total military expenditure by all governments, on the lines about to be explored by the United Nations.

3. FOR RESOLVING WORLD PROBLEMS AND STRENGTHENING THE UNITED NATIONS

3.1 Reaffirmation by all governments of their adherence to the obligations, taken by them under the Charter, to the United Nations, as the highest world authority, and recognition by them of the need to strengthen and use its peace-making machinery to the full in resolving international disputes, to develop a rule of international law and to create conditions in which states feel it is safe to disarm.

3.2 The full implementation of the Non-Proliferation Treaty and the strengthening of the international non-proliferation regime through the implementation by the nuclear powers of the clause requiring a reduction of their nuclear armaments.

3.3 The immediate conclusion of an international convention banning the production, stockpiling and use of chemical weapons.

3.4 The adoption of measures to reduce the international arms-trade.

3.5 The development of appropriate provisions for the verification of all arms control and disarmament measures.

3.6 Co-operation with and financial contribution to the United Nations World Disarmament Campaign for the distribution of information and educational material on disarmament matters, by governments and non-governmental organisations.

3.7 Recognition of the right of conscientious objection to military service.

3.8 Acceptance of the integrity, free from foreign intervention, of nation states within frontiers recognised by the United Nations.

3.9 Reaffirmation by all states of the founding declaration of the United Nations that war is no longer an acceptable means of resolving international conflict.

3.10 Acceptance and endorsement of the UN Convention on the Law of the Sea proclaiming the international sea-bed the "common heritage of mankind".

3.11 The transformation of the Indian Ocean and the South Pacific into zones of peace, free of nuclear weapons and their transit, and further progressive demilitarisation of the oceans.

3.12 The rehabilitation of islands in the Pacific and other territories used for nuclear weapons testing.

3.13 Reaffirmation, on a permanent basis, of the Antarctic Treaty (due to expire in 1989), to ensure that the Antarctic remains free of military installations and uncontrolled exploitation for all time.

4. FOR DISARMAMENT AND DEVELOPMENT

4.1 The progressive transfer to civil development, particularly in third world countries, of the resources now being used for military purposes.

4.2 An agreement by all nations to devote immediately 1% of their current military budgets to set up an international fund for long term developments – for example, the improvement of global drinking water supplies.

4.3 Greater co-operation between developed and developing countries in the fields of disarmament and development, including the establishment of a New International Economic Order. This should be linked with the solution of the immediate and urgent problems.

4.4 The development of plans, in co-operation with the industries concerned, for the conversion of military industries to the production of socially useful products.

4.5 The initiation of global measures to prevent further deterioration of the world eco-system and to encourage an "ecological" perspective on world affairs and acceptance of the recommendation of the Stockholm conference, 1982, that "states are responsible for avoiding damage to the environment of other states or of the International Realm".

This document has been prepared as a basis for common campaigning, following discussion with Peace Movements all over the world. The aims embodied in this programme for a peaceful world will be achieved not only by influencing governments to implement it, but also by developing co-operation between peoples based on understanding, friendship and good will. It is the immediate purpose of the programme to help bring about such co-operation by encouraging peace movements internationally to develop links with each other and to share a common approach to disarmament. Letters of support for the programme, along with suggestions for its realisation, will be welcomed.

June 1985

Published by World Disarmament Campaign (UK),
238 Camden Road,
London NW1 9HE.
United Kingdom.

design: Skater

A Speech Delivered in the House of Lords
22 October 1985

Nuclear Armaments

Lord Brockway rose to ask Her Majesty's Government whether they will take the initiative towards securing the international signature of a comprehensive ban on all nuclear tests as proposed in the preamble to the non-proliferation treaty, and whether they will revitalize that treaty by discussing with the nuclear arms-holding countries the substantial reduction of their nuclear armaments.
The noble Lord said:

My Lords, I beg leave to ask the Question standing in my name on the Order Paper. The non-proliferation treaty is the most hopeful treaty signed in recent years. It is the world's only multilateral treaty aimed at halting both the spread and the build-up of nuclear weapons. Its provisions were, first, that the non-nuclear signatories agreed not to develop or acquire nuclear weapons; secondly, that the nuclear states:

> undertook to pursue negotiations in good faith on effective measures relating to cessation of the nuclear arms race at an early date and to nuclear disarmament - and on a treaty on general and complete disarmament under strict and effective international control.

Its third provision was that all signatories agreed:

> to seek to achieve the discontinuance of all test explosions of nuclear weapons for all time and to continue negotiations to this end.

The fourth provision was that all parties agreed that the object of the treaty would be realized:

> under appropriate international observation, thus accepting the principle of verification.

These momentous decisions were reached by 130 nations, including the United States, the Soviet Union and Great Britain, and by 124 non-nuclear States. There is no evidence that the non-nuclear states have not carried out their obligations under the treaty. Unhappily, there is abundant evidence that the nuclear powers have not done so. They agreed that they would pursue negotiations relating to the cessation of the nuclear arms race at an early date and to nuclear disarmament.

In fact, the total number of strategic nuclear weapons has risen from 6,000 in 1970 – the year the NPT came into force – to 20,000 this year. Acceleration has taken place not only in the numbers but in their destructive force. The Committee of World Scientists five years ago reported to the United Nations that a bomb had been created 4,000 – 4,000! – times as deadly as the bomb which fell on Hiroshima.

As for general and complete disarmament, the United States and the United Kingdom have sought to kill the comprehensive disarmament programme proposed by the Committee on disarmament at Geneva. The non-nuclear states are furious at this failure. I have spoken to a number of them and have been impressed by the depth of their despair. They say, 'Why should we join the NPT when the super-powers repudiate it by expanding their nuclear arms?'

The opposition of the non-nuclear states to accepting the NPT was expressed vigorously at the third review of the treaty held in September. Importantly, they accompanied their criticism with a call to the nuclear states to conclude a comprehensive test ban treaty. There was no accepted communiqué, but the final consensus document, while stating that the objective of nuclear disarmament remained unfulfilled, called emphatically for the resumption of negotiations this year on a comprehensive test ban treaty. Speech after speech emphasized this. It is not too much to say that this is the way to save the Non-Proliferation Treaty. If it is not done, the NPT will be killed at the fourth review, which will be a terrible tragedy.

My Lords, there is hope. The United States of America, the Soviet Union, and the United Kingdom accept in this treaty the necessity for a comprehensive test ban treaty. The Senate of the United States has called on President Reagan to negotiate. The Soviet Union has proposed a moratorium. The United States of America and the United Kingdom say that the difficulty is verification. This treaty accepts the need for international observation. Scientists say overwhelmingly that verification is now possible. The Soviet Union has gone far to accept it.

One cannot avoid the conclusion that it is political will rather than technology which is holding up verification. I beg the Government to act. Their conscience will not be easy if failure to do so destroys this treaty; this treaty of hope for ending the fear of a nuclear war.

Curriculum

1888	1 November, born in Calcutta. Parents Christian missionaries
1903	At School for the Sons of Missionaries (now Eltham College) Became pro-Boer in South African war
1905	Joined the Young Liberals
1906	Liberal sub-agent at the general election at Tunbridge Wells
1907	From a settlement in a slum in Islington campaigned for benefits for the unemployed, school meals for hungry children, and wages councils for sweated home workers, giving evidence of their conditions. Converted to Socialism by Keir Hardie, founder of the Labour Party, particularly attracted by his anti-militarism Joined staff of the *Examiner*
1909	Sub-editor of the *Christian Commonwealth*, organ of a rational theology, democratic Socialism and peace
1909	Stood as Labour candidate for Finsbury Borough Council on his 21st birthday. Defeated by 30 votes. (In all he stood as a Parliamentary candidate eleven times in seven constituencies, four times for the ILP and seven times for the Labour Party. As recorded below, he was elected for East Leyton and Eton and Slough)
1910	Campaigned for women's suffrage, leaving the WSPU when it resorted to violence

and joining the National Union of Women's Suffrage Societies

1911-17 Editor of the *Labour Leader*, organ of the Independent Labour Party (ILP)

1914 Married Lilla Harvey-Smith (four daughters: Audrey, Margaret, Joan, Olive)

1915 Exchanged letters through Sweden with Rosa Luxemburg and Karl Liebknecht and anti-war movement in Germany. Formed the No-Conscription Fellowship of 6,000 young men who declined to serve in the military forces

1916-19 Sentenced to imprisonment for one month, six months, twelve months and two years for opposing conscription and refusing to obey military orders

1919 Welcomed, when free, the Soviet Revolution but criticized its Authoritarianism
Joint Secretary of British Committee of the Indian National Congress
Editor of *India*

1920 Joint Secretary of the Prison System Enquiry

1922 Organizing Secretary of the ILP

1923 Chairman of War Resisters International and the No More War movement

1926-9 Editor of the *New Leader*, renamed organ of the ILP. Moved resolution at Labour Party Conference committing the Party to independence for India. ILP representative on the Executive Committee of the Socialist International, speaking in Germany, Belgium, Austria, France and Switzerland

1927 Invited to Indian National Congress Conference by Mahatma Gandhi and Jawaharlal Nehru. Attended Indian Trades Union Congress, but broke thigh in motor accident on eve of Conference.

1928 First chairman of the League Against Imperialism, uniting Asian and African leaders with European opponents of imperialism

1928 General-Secretary of ILP (also 1933–9)

1929–31 Labour MP for East Leyton. Member of ILP's 'Group of Seventeen' which became the opposition to Ramsay MacDonald's policy. Spoke particularly on disarmament and peace. Visited USA and Canada three times on lecture tours for League for Industrial Democracy

1930 Did research for Mahatma Gandhi on non-violent Non-Co-operation, published in Madras as *Non-Co-operation in Other Lands*. Wore Gandhi cap in House of Commons when protesting against arrests of Indians for wearing it. Suspended from Commons when protesting against the arrest of Gandhi, Nehru and 6000 Congressmen

1931 Chairman of International Bureau of socialist parties not affiliated to Social Democratic and Communist Internationals

Visited Poland and Germany

1931–3 Chairman of ILP, which disaffiliated from the Labour Party, claiming that MPs should have the right to vote according to their conscience. ILP led opposition to Fascism. Organized mass blockade in East London to stop Mosely march in Jewish area. March stopped after clash with Communists

1936 Organized ILP contingent to fight against Franco in Spain

1937 Went to Spain, ironically, to rescue ILP volunteers, including George Orwell, from Communists

1938 Urged ILP to reaffiliate with Labour Party

1938–45 Differed with ILP National Council's support of the Munich Agreement. During the war concentrated on urging a Peace Treaty which would prevent a recurrence of war and on a democratic Socialist transformation

1942–47 Chairman of the British Centre for Colonial Freedom

1945 Established with French anti-imperialists the Congress of Peoples Against Imperialism, uniting Europeans with Asian and African Nationalist leaders

1946 Married Edith King (one son, Christopher) Chairman of Congress of Peoples against Imperialism
Fraternal Delegate to Hamburg Trade Union May Day

1947 Presented with a Tunisian decoration for services to peace

1950–64 Elected as Labour MP for Eton and Slough

1950 Visited Uganda and Kenya

1954–67 When British Centre for Colonial Freedom disbanded, established in Britain the Movement for Colonial Freedom, which became a major pressure group. It was succeeded by Liberation, of which he became President

1951 Fraternal Delegate to Tunisian Trade Union Conference (via Switzerland)

1952 Visited Kenya on unofficial fact-finding tour. Advice on ending Mau Mau accepted

1954 Visited Madagascar. (Discovered grandfather was hero among dissidents because, as a non-conformist missionary, he had criticized the Catholic dictatorship of the French.) Ordered to leave after three days although ill with fever. Went to Mauritius to the house of Dr Remgoolan, Prime Minister and medical practitioner. Quickly recovered

1956 Went to Athens with Leon Szur to Conference on West Bank attended by Israelis and Palestinians

1957 Went to Athens with Parliamentary Labour Party delegation to negotiate future of Cyprus with the Greek Government

1959-66 British Asian and Overseas Socialist Fellowship

1964 Defeated in General Election by eleven votes, largely on the racial issue. Appointed to the House of Lords as a life Peer, as Baron Brockway of Eton and Slough. Until disabled by deafness, put more Questions, introduced more Bills and initiated more debates than any other back-bencher

1965 Went to conference at Florence on Israeli/Arab relations called by the Florentine Mayor

1965-9 Initiated and became chairman of the British Committee for Peace in Vietnam

1967-70 Initiated and became chairman of the all-party and all-churches Committee for peace in Nigeria. Went with James Griffiths to Biafra and Lagos and negotiated a truce and sought to extend it to peace

1975 Went to Cyprus, accompanied by son Christopher, to negotiate with Archbishop Makarios

1978 Visited East Africa for talks with Presidents Kaunda and Nyerere and Prime Minister Moi. Visited India to lecture and speak in New Delhi and Bombay

1979-86 With Lord Philip Noel-Baker established the World Disarmament Campaign (later

WDC [UK]) to secure the implementation of the recommendations of the first UN Special Session on Disarmament (1978). Became founding Co-Chairman. After the death of Noel-Baker, co-chaired with Rev Kenneth Greet

1980 Presented with a Vietnamese order for services for peace

1982 Lancaster University conferred honorary degree of Doctor of Law

Attended Second Special Session on Disarmament in New York, presenting petition of over 2 million signatures to UN Sec-General

Attended conference at Brussels under auspices of END and Bertrand Russell Peace Foundation on West-East Relations. Accompanied Northern Friends Peace Board to Moscow, which endorsed his draft for a Peace Programme for submission to the Soviet Peace Committee Accepted, with minor amendments

1983 Attended World Conference for Peace and Life, Prague. Negotiated extensions to World Peace Action Programme and signatures

Visited USA to assist in the development of the Bharatiya Vidya Bhavan. Lectured on Gandhi at Boston University

1983-5 WPAP extended in Britain, sent out nationally and internationally and extensively endorsed. Major launch November 1985

Attended peace conferences and NGO meetings in Geneva (3 times), Athens, Berlin, Perugia, Stockholm, Helsinki, lobbying for WPAP and a World Conference

1984 Invited by the Buddhist order, Nipponzan

Myohoji, to 100th birthday of Most Venerable Fujii, in Tokyo. Visited Hiroshima for A and H Bomb Conference and for anniversary. Consultations with Japanese statesmen. Taken ill, with sunstroke. On to India at invitation of Indira Gandhi for discussions on a possible World Peace Conference in Delhi, in 1986. Attended Indian Independence Day celebrations

1985 Invited to attend 100th Anniversary of Indian Congress in December. Presented with Indian Congress Medal by Rajiv Gandhi

1986 Appointed President of Labour CND
Resigned Co-Chairmanship of WDC (UK) in May. Elected President

Index

R.T.C. LIBRARY, LETTERKENNY